Laser Cooling of Solids: Novel Advances and Applications

Laser Cooling of Solids: Novel Advances and Applications

Editor

Galina Nemova

MDPI • Basel • Beijing • Wuhan • Barcelona • Belgrade • Manchester • Tokyo • Cluj • Tianjin

Editor
Galina Nemova
Polytechnique Montréal
Canada

Editorial Office
MDPI
St. Alban-Anlage 66
4052 Basel, Switzerland

This is a reprint of articles from the Special Issue published online in the open access journal *Applied Sciences* (ISSN 2076-3417) (available at: https://www.mdpi.com/journal/applsci/special_issues/Laser_Cooling_Solids).

For citation purposes, cite each article independently as indicated on the article page online and as indicated below:

LastName, A.A.; LastName, B.B.; LastName, C.C. Article Title. *Journal Name* **Year**, *Volume Number*, Page Range.

ISBN 978-3-0365-5079-4 (Hbk)
ISBN 978-3-0365-5080-0 (PDF)

© 2022 by the authors. Articles in this book are Open Access and distributed under the Creative Commons Attribution (CC BY) license, which allows users to download, copy and build upon published articles, as long as the author and publisher are properly credited, which ensures maximum dissemination and a wider impact of our publications.
The book as a whole is distributed by MDPI under the terms and conditions of the Creative Commons license CC BY-NC-ND.

Contents

About the Editor vii

Preface to "Laser Cooling of Solids: Novel Advances and Applications" ix

Galina Nemova
Editorial for the Special Issue: "Laser Cooling of Solids: Novel Advances and Applications"
Reprinted from: *Appl. Sci.* **2022**, *12*, 7951, doi:10.3390/app12157951 1

Galina Nemova
Radiation-Balanced Lasers: History, Status, Potential
Reprinted from: *Appl. Sci.* **2021**, *11*, 7539, doi:10.3390/app11167539 3

Elena A. Dobretsova, Anupum Pant, Xiaojing Xia, Rachel E. Gariepy and Peter J. Pauzauskie
Safe and Scalable Polyethylene Glycol-Assisted Hydrothermal Synthesis and Laser Cooling of 10%Yb^{3+}:$LiLuF_4$ Crystals
Reprinted from: *Appl. Sci.* **2022**, *12*, 774, doi:10.3390/app12020774 27

Xuelu Duan, Biao Zhong, Yongqing Lei, Chaoyu Wang, Jiajin Xu, Ziheng Zhang, Jingxin Ding and Jianping Yin
Accurate Characterization of the Properties of the Rare-Earth-Doped Crystal for Laser Cooling
Reprinted from: *Appl. Sci.* **2022**, *12*, 4447, doi:10.3390/app12094447 35

Laura B. Andre, Long Cheng and Stephen C. Rand
Saturation, Allowed Transitions and Quantum Interference in Laser Cooling of Solids
Reprinted from: *Appl. Sci.* **2022**, *12*, 953, doi:10.3390/app12030953 45

Conor N. Murphy, Luísa Toledo Tude and Paul R. Eastham
Laser Cooling beyond Rate Equations: Approaches from Quantum Thermodynamics
Reprinted from: *Appl. Sci.* **2022**, *12*, 1620, doi:10.3390/app12031620 71

About the Editor

Galina Nemova

Dr. Galina Nemova is a research fellow at Polytechnique Montréal. She received her M.Sc. and Ph.D. degrees from the Moscow Institute of Physics and Technology. Dr. Nemova is a Senior Member of Optica, formerly the Optical Society of America. She has edited two books and authored more than 100 papers. She is the author of *Field Guide to Laser Cooling Methods* (2019) and *Field Guide to Light-Matter Interaction* (2022). Her research interests cover a broad range of photonics topics, including rare-earth-doped materials, nanophotonics, fiber lasers and amplifiers, Raman lasers, nonlinear optics, and laser cooling of solids.

Preface to "Laser Cooling of Solids: Novel Advances and Applications"

Cooling or refrigeration is a physical process in which a substance is maintained at a temperature below that of its surroundings. It has a long history and dates back thousands of years when people used ice and snow in order to preserve their food. Laser cooling of solids is a research area investigating the interaction of light with condensed matter resulting in the cooling of solids. It is based on anti-Stokes fluorescence discovered at the beginning of the 20th century. This book brings together the latest achievements and applications of laser cooling solids, including heat mitigation in high power lasers (Chapter 1), synthesis and laser cooling of 10%Yb^{3+}:$LiLuF_4$ crystals (Chapter 2), characterization of the properties of rare-earth-doped crystals for laser cooling (Chapter 3), quantum interference in laser cooling of solids (Chapter 4). The use of Bloch–Redfield equations to model laser cooling are considered in Chapter 5. It is hoped that continuous progress in the laser cooling of solids will soon result in the development of new optical refrigerating devices for different applications.

Galina Nemova
Editor

Editorial

Editorial for the Special Issue: "Laser Cooling of Solids: Novel Advances and Applications"

Galina Nemova

Polytechnique Montréal, 2500 ch. de Polytechnique, Montréal, QC H3T 1J4, Canada; galina.nemova@videotron.ca

Laser cooling, or refrigeration, is a physical process in which a substance is maintained at a temperature below that of its surroundings. The process dates back thousands of years to when people attempted to preserve their food using ice and snow placed in holes in the ground or in cold cellars. In the 19th century, scientists liquefied the permanent gases and brought cryogenics into existence. In 1929, Pringsheim proposed to use anti-Stokes fluorescence to cool sodium vapor [1]. In his "theoretical" experiment, the sodium vapor in "Dewar 1" was pumped with a filtered sodium vapor lamp in order to excite electrons from the $^2S_{1/2}$ ground state to the first $^2P_{1/2}$ excited state (Figure 1). Inelastic collisions in the gas (thermalization) excite some electrons to $^2P_{3/2}$ excited state. The excited electrons relax to the ground state with resonant and anti-Stokes fluorescence, thus removing energy from the system and causing its refrigeration. This fluorescence has to be quenched by nonradiative relaxation with heat generation in "Dewar 2" filled with the mixture of sodium vapor and nitrogen.

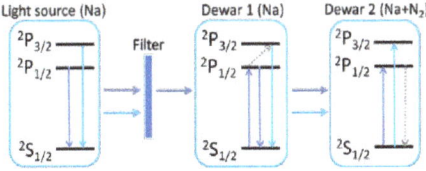

Figure 1. Pringsheim's experiment.

In 1960, the first laser was demonstrated. This groundbreaking scientific achievement has revolutionized optical cooling with anti-Stokes fluorescence. In 1995, optical cooling with anti-stokes fluorescence was demonstrated for a rare-earth-doped solid pumped with a laser [2]; thus, laser cooling of solids with anti-Stokes fluorescence was born. In this first experiment, a high-purity ytterbium (Yb^{3+})-doped fluorozirconate ZrF_4-BaF_2-LaF_3-AlF_3-NaF-PbF_2 (ZBLANP) glass sample was cooled down to only 0.3 K below room temperature. In the last two decades, laser cooling of solids progressed rapidly.

This Special Issue presents the latest advances in laser cooling of solids and its applications in different scientific fields.

The replacement of flash-lamps by laser-diode pumping for solid-state lasers has improved the laser technology. Compared to flash-lamp pumps, the use of laser diodes has led to significant benefits in efficiency, simplicity, compactness, reliability and cost. At the same time, the thermal problem has come into existence for high power lasers. Indeed, in the majority of lasers, heat generated inside the laser medium is an unavoidable product of the lasing process. Different approaches including fiber lasers and thin-disk lasers were developed in order to mitigate heat in lasers. The idea of radiation-balanced (athermal) lasers operating without detrimental heating of laser medium was presented by Nemova G. in review [3]. This new design of optically pumped rare-earth-doped solid-state lasers is based on the principle of anti-Stokes fluorescence cooling of the laser medium. The

Citation: Nemova, G. Editorial for the Special Issue: "Laser Cooling of Solids: Novel Advances and Applications". *Appl. Sci.* **2022**, *12*, 7951. https://doi.org/10.3390/app12157951

Received: 22 July 2022
Accepted: 2 August 2022
Published: 8 August 2022

Publisher's Note: MDPI stays neutral with regard to jurisdictional claims in published maps and institutional affiliations.

Copyright: © 2022 by the author. Licensee MDPI, Basel, Switzerland. This article is an open access article distributed under the terms and conditions of the Creative Commons Attribution (CC BY) license (https://creativecommons.org/licenses/by/4.0/).

review is devoted to the history and progress on radiation-balanced lasers with a special focus on rare-earth-doped lasers. Four main designs of athermal lasers including radiation-balanced bulk and fiber lasers, radiation-balanced disk lasers, and athermal microlasers have been considered.

Dobretsova E.A. et al. [4] describe synthesis and laser cooling of 10%Yb^{3+}:LiLuF$_4$ crystals. The 10%Yb^{3+}:LiLuF$_4$ (Yb:LLF) crystals have been synthesized through a safe and scalable polyethylene glycol (PEG)-assisted hydrothermal method. The influence of reaction temperature, time, fluoride source, and precursor amount on the shape and size of the Yb:LLF crystals are discussed in the paper. Laser cooling to more than 15 K below room temperature in air and 5 K in deionized water under 1020 nm diode laser excitation have been demonstrated at a laser power of 50 mW.

New methods for the rapid cooling of solids with increased efficiency have been analyzed and demonstrated experimentally by Andre L.B. et al. [5]. The advances offered by optical saturation, dipole-allowed transitions, and quantum interference for improved laser cooling of solids have been comprehensively discussed in this paper.

Murphy, C. et al. [6] review the derivation of the Bloch-Redfield equation for a quantum system coupled to a reservoir, and its extension, using counting fields to calculate heat current. They use the full form of this equation, which makes only weak-coupling and Markovian approximations, to calculate the cooling power for a simple model of laser cooling.

Two parameters, namely, the external quantum efficiency η_{ext} and the background absorption coefficient α_b, are important for assessing the laser cooling grade of the rare-earth-doped materials. A promising method for measuring of these crucial parameters has been presented by Duan X. et al. [7]. After calibration, the temperature resolution of the thermal camera was better than 0.1 K.

To conclude, this Special Issue, "Laser Cooling of Solids: Novel Advances and Applications", includes research and review papers that present the latest achievements on the subject. The data presented may be of great interest for a better understanding and application of the laser cooling of solids based on anti-Stokes fluorescence.

Funding: This research received no external funding.

Conflicts of Interest: The author declares no conflict of interest.

Short Biography of Author

Dr. Galina Nemova is a research fellow at Polytechnique Montréal. She received her M.Sc. and Ph.D. degrees from the Moscow Institute of Physics and Technology. Dr. Nemova is a Senior Member of Optica, formerly the Optical Society of America. She has edited two books and authored more than 100 papers. She is the author of *Field Guide to Laser Cooling Methods* (2019) *and Field Guide to Light–Matter Interaction* (2022). Her research interests cover a broad range of photonics topics, including rare-earth-doped materials, nanophotonics, fiber lasers and amplifiers, Raman lasers, nonlinear optics, and laser cooling of solids.

References

1. Pringsheim, P. Zwei Bemerkungen über den Unterschied von Lumineszenz- und Temperaturstrahlung. *Z. Phys.* **1929**, *57*, 739–746. [CrossRef]
2. Epstein, R.I.; Buchwald, M.I.; Edwards, B.C.; Gosnell, T.R.; Mungan, C.E. Observation of laser-induced fluorescent cooling of a solid. *Nature* **1995**, *377*, 500–502. [CrossRef]
3. Nemova, G. Radiation-Balanced Lasers: History, Status, Potential. *Appl. Sci.* **2021**, *11*, 7539. [CrossRef]
4. Dobretsova, E.; Pant, A.; Xia, X.; Gariepy, R.; Pauzauskie, P. Safe and Scalable Polyethylene Glycol-Assisted Hydrothermal Synthesis and Laser Cooling of 10%Yb^{3+}:LiLuF$_4$ Crystals. *Appl. Sci.* **2022**, *12*, 774. [CrossRef]
5. Andre, L.; Cheng, L.; Rand, S. Saturation, Allowed Transitions and Quantum Interference in Laser Cooling of Solids. *Appl. Sci.* **2022**, *12*, 953. [CrossRef]
6. Murphy, C.; Toledo Tude, L.; Eastham, P. Laser Cooling beyond Rate Equations: Approaches from Quantum Thermodynamics. *Appl. Sci.* **2022**, *12*, 1620. [CrossRef]
7. Duan, X.; Zhong, B.; Lei, Y.; Wang, C.; Xu, J.; Zhang, Z.; Ding, J.; Yin, J. Accurate Characterization of the Properties of the Rare-Earth-Doped Crystal for Laser Cooling. *Appl. Sci.* **2022**, *12*, 4447. [CrossRef]

Review

Radiation-Balanced Lasers: History, Status, Potential

Galina Nemova

Department of Electrical Engineering, Polytechnique Montréal, 2500 ch. de Polytechnique, Montréal, QC H3T 1H4, Canada; galina.nemova@videotron.ca

Abstract: The review of history and progress on radiation-balanced (athermal) lasers is presented with a special focus on rare earth (RE)-doped lasers. In the majority of lasers, heat generated inside the laser medium is an unavoidable product of the lasing process. Radiation-balanced lasers can provide lasing without detrimental heating of laser medium. This new approach to the design of optically pumped RE-doped solid-state lasers is provided by balancing the spontaneous and stimulated emission within the laser medium. It is based on the principle of anti-Stokes fluorescence cooling of RE-doped low-phonon solids. The theoretical description of the operation of radiation-balanced lasers based on the set of coupled rate equations is presented and discussed. It is shown that, for athermal operation, the value of the pump wavelength of the laser must exceed the value of the mean fluorescence wavelength of the RE laser active ions doped in the laser medium. The improved purity of host crystals and better control of the transverse intensity profile will result in improved performance of the radiation-balanced laser. Recent experimental achievements in the development of radiation-balanced RE-doped bulk lasers, fibre lasers, disk lasers, and microlasers are reviewed and discussed.

Keywords: radiation-balanced lasers; athermal lasers; solid-state lasers; laser cooling of solids; rare earth-doped materials

1. Introduction

The replacement of flash lamps by laser-diode pumping for solid-state lasers has brought a very important breakthrough in the laser technology, in particular for high-power lasers [1,2]. Compared to flash-lamp pumps, laser diodes have led to a significant benefit in efficiency, simplicity, compactness, reliability, and cost. At the same time the thermal problem has come into existence for high power lasers. Special care concerning thermal management is necessary to develop efficient high-power lasers.

To solve the thermal problem, the classical rod solid-state laser medium design has been replaced by new approaches including fibre lasers, slab lasers, and thin-disk lasers. The very high surface-to-volume ratio and optical guidance have provided tremendous progress in the power scalability of high-power lasers.

The benefit of using a rare earth (RE)-doped single-mode optical fibre as a laser medium was realized by Snitzer in 1961 [3]. In this paper, the use of fibres as dielectric waveguides to provide a resonant structure for an optical maser operating in the 0.6 μm wavelength region was proposed. In the mid-1980s, research of single-mode optical fibre lasers was carried out very intensively [4–7]. A decade later, fibre structures with large mode areas based on multimode optical fibres were proposed to solve the problem [8]. The schemes, in which the amplification takes place in an RE-doped fibre cladding, have been proposed as a solution of the problem as well [9]. Unfortunately, even these schemes are limited by thermal lensing if a high-quality beam is required. Water cooling is not suitable for fibres with limited chemical stability, such as fluoride fibres. Lowering of the dopant concentration and increasing the length of the fibre makes cooling easier, but increases the chance of nonlinear effects including stimulated Brillouin scattering (SBS) and stimulated Raman scattering (SRS), which result in depletion of the amplified signal in ion-doped lasers.

In 1972, Martin and Chernock [10] proposed a new approach to the development of solid-state lasers. It is based on the idea of propagating laser beams in a direction that averages the temperature gradients in the gain medium [11]. The laser beam is injected into the slab so that it will allow the beam to make multiple total internal reflections from the polished sides as it propagates down the slab.

In 1991, Giesen et al. proposed to power a scale Yb^{3+}:YAG laser using a thin-disk laser design. The first thin-disk laser was demonstrated in 1994 [12,13]. The core concept of the thin-disk lasers is the use of a thin, disk-shaped active medium that is cooled through one of the flat faces of the disk. The cooled face is used as a mirror of the resonator. This face cooling minimizes the transversal temperature gradient, as well as the phase distortion transversal to the direction of the beam propagation, providing a laser beam of outstanding quality.

In 1999, Bowman [14] proposed a radiation-balanced (athermal) RE-doped bulk laser, which operates *without* internal heating. In this laser, all photons generated in the laser cycle are annihilated with the cooling cycle, that is, the heat generated from stimulated emission is offset by cooling from anti-Stokes emission. Athermal lasers, which are free from all thermal effects, provide a tremendous potential for an increase in the output power, maintaining a high-quality output laser beam. Beginning in 1999, several kinds of radiation-balanced lasers, including fibre lasers, disk lasers, and microlasers, have been proposed and developed. Some of these lasers have been discussed in [15], while others are considered in this review. Thermal lensing arising in traditional lasers from the quantum-defect heating is briefly discussed in Section 2. Section 3 is devoted to the theory of radiation-balanced lasing. Recent achievements in the development of radiation-balanced RE-doped bulk lasers, fibre lasers, disk lasers, and microlasers are presented in Section 4.

2. Laser Heat Management

Most materials are not optically active. They simply convert absorbed laser power directly into heat. If α_a is an absorption coefficient describing the absorption process and I_L is the laser intensity, the absorbed power density is equal to $\alpha_a I_L$. This is not the case for laser media, which are optically active. The laser performance is based on efficient reemitting of absorbed pump light. The amount of heat generated in a laser depends on the pump power and the emission spectra.

It is well known that population inversion is a necessary condition for lasing. It is impossible to reach the population inversion in a two-level system. Three or four level schemes are required. As a result, the reradiated light is normally red-shifted relative to the pump (Figure 1).

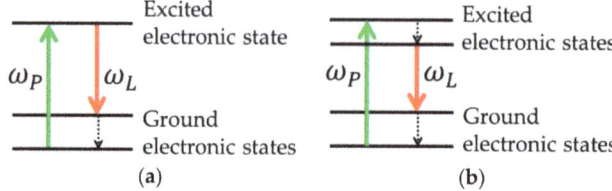

Figure 1. Energy levels and relevant excitation and decay processes for (**a**) three-level and (**b**) four-level lasers.

By this means, every emitted laser photon contributes a fraction of its energy,

$$\eta_{QD} = 1 - \omega_L/\omega_P, \tag{1}$$

to heating the laser material through phonon generation. Here η_{QD} is the quantum defect, ω_P and ω_L are the frequencies of the pump and laser photons, respectively.

A study of thermal effects in a crystal requires the calculation of the temperature field at each point of the crystal. This can be achieved with the heat equation. For analytical solutions to the heat equation to be obtained, some assumptions must be imposed on the laser system. Let us suppose that the pump profile is axisymmetric, and the thermal conductivity of the laser medium does not depend on temperature and can be considered as a constant. In this case, the heat equation has the form [16]:

$$\frac{1}{r}\frac{\partial}{\partial r}\left(r\frac{\partial T}{\partial r}\right) + \frac{\partial^2 T}{\partial r^2} = -\frac{Q}{K_c}, \quad (2)$$

where T is the temperature, r is the radial coordinate of a point inside the laser medium (see insert in Figure 2), K_c is the thermal conductivity, and Q is the thermal power.

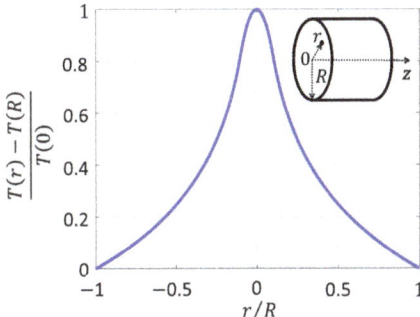

Figure 2. Normalized temperature distribution in a plane perpendicular to the z-axis for a laser medium pumped by a top-hat-profile laser beam. Inset is the laser medium with the radius R.

In a vast majority of laser schemes, the pump beam profile can be described by a super-Gaussian function. The general solution of the heat Equation (2) for a super-Gaussian beam of any order, as well as for Gaussian and top-hat pump beams, can be found in [17–20]. As one can see in these solutions, heat generated in the laser's interior produces a temperature rise in the center of the laser medium relative to its edge. As an example, normalized temperature distribution for a laser crystal pumped by a top-hat-profile pump beam is presented in Figure 2.

The temperature rise in the laser medium produces several undesirable effects. It reduces the lifetime of the laser active ions and increases losses. The temperature gradient causes the strain distribution inside the laser medium. The strain-induced modification of the refractive index results in depolarization and degradation in beam quality. It limits the average laser output power [21]. All these effects are known as thermal lensing. They are particularly important in the case of high-power lasers. The very high temperature rise can even melt or burn the laser medium (thermal damage). In most laser structures, beam quality degradation limits laser power below thermal damage.

As mentioned earlier, the problem of laser power scaling can be solved by reducing or eliminating the heat generated during the optical pumping and lasing process using optical cooling by anti-Stokes fluorescence within the laser medium to balance the heat generated by the Stokes shifted stimulated emission. The theory of this approach is considered in the next section.

3. Theory of Radiation-Balanced Lasing

In this part of the paper, I develop a model permitting to investigate the fundamental limitations of laser thermal performances. Let us consider a quasi-three-level material in which radiative losses dominate at room temperature emission and absorption spectra overlap near the lasing wavelength. This requirement is a critical material characteristic for a potential radiation-balanced laser. Indeed, there must be a sufficiently strong absorption in the spectral region near the lasing wavelength to allow effective coupling of the pump.

As one can see in Equation (1) as the frequency of the pump, ω_P, approaches the frequency of the laser signal, ω_L, the quantum defect reduces, and the heat power generated by spontaneous emission reduces, too. A minimum value for the laser quantum defect can be estimated as $k_B T/\hbar \omega_P$. It corresponds to the least amount of heat power generated by the stimulated emission providing laser operation. Let us take into account spontaneous fluorescence. Its power cannot be neglected unless the average stimulated emission rate far exceeds the rate of spontaneous emission. Spontaneous fluorescence of the laser medium can contribute significantly to radiation power flow. In certain situations, it can lead to cooling which can compensate for the laser induced heating.

3.1. Pringsheim's Cooling

The idea to remove the thermal energy from a system optically using anti-Stokes fluorescence was first proposed by Pringsheim in 1929 [22]. In 1995, laser cooling with anti-Stokes fluorescence was demonstrated for RE-doped solids [23]. In this first proof-of-principle experiment, a high-purity ytterbium (Yb^{3+})-doped fluorozirconate ZrF_4–BaF_2–LaF_3–AlF_3–NaF–PbF_2 (ZBLANP) glass sample was cooled down to only 0.3 K below room temperature.

Each energy level of the RE ions doped into the crystal or glass host splits into a set of sublevels as a result of the Stark effect. These sets of sublevels are known as Stark level manifolds. In order to realize cooling with anti-Stokes fluorescence in an RE-doped sample, electrons must be excited from the top of the ground manifold to the bottom of the excited manifold of the RE ions. This implies that the pump wavelength, $\lambda_P = 2\pi c/\omega_P$, must be in the long wavelength tail of the absorption spectrum. After thermalization accompanied by phonon absorption, anti-Stokes fluorescence photons remove energy from the system (Figure 3).

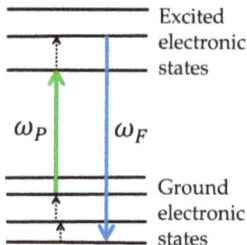

Figure 3. Energy levels and relevant excitation and decay processes for the laser-cooled RE-doped sample. ω_P and ω_F are the pump and the mean fluorescence frequencies, respectively.

The efficiency of laser cooling can be estimated as a difference between the energy of the mean fluorescence photon, $\hbar\omega_F$, and the energy of the pump photon, $\hbar\omega_P$, normalized by the energy of the pump photon [24]:

$$\eta_{cool} = \frac{\hbar\omega_F - \hbar\omega_P}{\hbar\omega_P} = \frac{\lambda_P}{\lambda_F} - 1, \qquad (3)$$

where ω_P and λ_P are the frequency and the wavelength of the pump photon, respectively.

$$\lambda_F = \frac{2\pi c}{\omega_F} = \frac{\int \lambda I_F(\lambda) d\lambda}{\int I_F(\lambda) d\lambda}, \qquad (4)$$

where λ_F and ω_F are the mean fluorescence wavelength and the mean fluorescence frequency, respectively. $I_F(\lambda)$ is the fluorescence intensity at the wavelength λ.

3.2. Athermal Lasing

As already mentioned, in 1999, Bowman [14] suggested to use cooling with anti-Stokes fluorescence to suppress heat generated in RE-doped solid-state lasers. He developed a new solid-state bulk laser design without internal heat generation called a radiation-balanced or athermal laser. The processes of lasing and anti-Stokes cooling in athermal lasers occur in the same system of RE ions. In 2001, Andrianov and Samartsev proposed a scheme in which lasing occurs in one system of ions (Nd^{3+}), while anti-Stokes cooling takes place in another system of ions (Yb^{3+}) doped in the KY_3F_{10} laser host [25].

3.2.1. Athermal Lasing in Ideal Systems

Let us consider the basic concepts of a radiation-balanced (athermal) laser. A solid-state laser of this type can be often referred to as a quasi-three-level laser. The population of each sublevel within a manifold is described by Boltzmann occupation factors. We assume that transitions between these sublevels are purely nonradiative transitions, provided by phonon absorption and emission. This process takes place on a picosecond timescale and is known as thermalization. Let us consider an isotropic laser medium with the total density of the active ions N_T. Optical transitions can occur between the ground manifold and the first excited manifolds, giving rise to overlapping, thermally broadened absorption and emission spectra. These spectra are characterized by absorption, $\sigma_a(\lambda, T)$, and emission, $\sigma_e(\lambda, T)$, cross sections, respectively. They depend on a wavelength, λ, and a temperature, T. For radiation-balanced operation of a laser, the mean fluorescence frequency and the pump and laser frequencies must satisfy the following relation: $\omega_F > \omega_P > \omega_L$ (Figure 4). In this case, the system includes two cycles: the laser cycle and the cooling cycle. The laser cycle includes the pump and laser photons at the frequencies ω_P and ω_L, respectively. It is accompanied by phonon generation. The cooling cycle can be considered as a cycle including the pump photon and the mean fluorescence photon at the frequencies ω_P and ω_F, respectively. It is accompanied by phonon absorption.

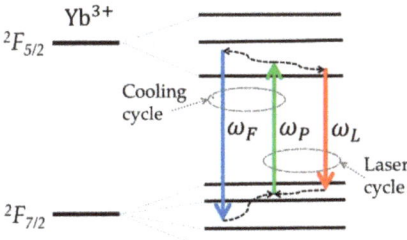

Figure 4. Energy diagram of an Yb^{3+}-doped radiation-balanced laser. ω_P and ω_L are the pump and laser frequencies, respectively. ω_F is the mean fluorescence frequency.

We assume that a bandgap between the excited and ground manifolds is large compared to the energies of the phonons. As a result, the transitions between the excited and ground manifolds are purely radiative. We also assume the absence of excited-state absorption, energy transfer, radiative trapping, and background absorption. In this case, the rate equation takes the form:

$$\frac{dN_2}{dt} = W_P - W_L - \frac{N_2}{\tau_R}, \tag{5}$$

$$N_1 + N_2 = N_T, \tag{6}$$

where N_1 is the population of the ground manifold and N_2 is the population of the excited manifold. The last term in Equation (5) describes the total spontaneous decay rate of the upper manifold. W_P is a pump rate, and W_L is the stimulated emission rate:

$$W_P = \frac{I_P}{\hbar \omega_P}\left[N_T \sigma_a^P - N_2\left(\sigma_a^P + \sigma_e^P\right)\right], \tag{7}$$

$$W_L = \frac{I_L}{\hbar \omega_L}\left[N_2\left(\sigma_a^L + \sigma_e^L\right) - N_T \sigma_a^L\right]. \tag{8}$$

Here I_P and I_L are the intensities of the pump beam and the laser signal, respectively. $\sigma_{a,e}^P$ and $\sigma_{a,e}^L$ are the absorption (a) and emission (e) cross sections at the pump (P) wavelength, λ_P, and at the laser (L) wavelength, λ_L, respectively.

Following the law of conservation of energy, one can estimate heat generated in the laser medium. Indeed, the difference between the absorbed power density and the emitted power density must be equal to the local generated heat power density:

$$P_{heat} = \hbar \omega_P W_P - \hbar \omega_L W_L - \hbar \omega_F \frac{N_2}{\tau_R} \tag{9}$$

Substituting Equations (5)–(8) into Equation (9), one can calculate the heat power density generated at any point of the laser medium. Equation (9) for heat power density includes both the pump, I_P, and laser, I_L, intensities in the laser medium.

If the laser system is in a steady state, $dN_2/dt = 0$, Equation (5) takes the form

$$W_P = W_L + \frac{N_2}{\tau_R} \tag{10}$$

Let us find the relation between the pump and laser beam intensities I_P and I_L providing athermal operation of the laser, $P_{heat} = 0$. In this case, Equation (9) becomes

$$\hbar \omega_P W_P = \hbar \omega_L W_L + \hbar \omega_F \frac{N_2}{\tau_R} \tag{11}$$

The change in the laser signal intensity along the length of the laser medium can be described by the well-known equation

$$\frac{dI_L}{dz} = \left[\left(\sigma_a^L + \sigma_e^L\right)N_2 - \sigma_a^L N_T\right]I_L, \tag{12}$$

where z is the coordinate along the length of the laser medium (see Insert in Figure 2). Substituting Equations (7)–(11) into Equation (12), one can obtain the equation, which describes the laser signal at any point, z, along the length of the laser medium

$$\frac{i_L(0)}{i_L(z)}exp(i_L(z) - i_L(0)) = exp\left(\sigma_a^L N_T z\right), \tag{13}$$

where $i_L(z) = I_L(z)/I_L^{sat}$, and $I_L^{sat} = \frac{\hbar \omega_L}{\tau(\sigma_a^L + \sigma_e^L)}\left(\frac{\omega_F - \omega_P}{\omega_P - \omega_L}\right)$ is the saturation intensity of the laser signal. To keep the radiation balance at each point in the laser medium, the pump intensity must be distributed properly along the length of the laser medium following the relation obtained from Equations (10) and (11)

$$i_P(z) = \frac{\sigma_a^L\left(\sigma_a^P + \sigma_e^P\right)i_L(z)}{\left(\sigma_a^P \sigma_e^L - \sigma_a^L \sigma_e^P\right)i_L(z) - \sigma_a^P\left(\sigma_a^L + \sigma_e^L\right)}, \tag{14}$$

where $i_P(z) = I_P(z)/I_P^{sat}$, and $I_P^{sat} = \frac{\hbar \omega_P}{\tau(\sigma_a^P + \sigma_e^P)}\left(\frac{\omega_F - \omega_L}{\omega_P - \omega_L}\right)$ is the saturation intensity of the pump signal. As one can see in Equation (14), athermal laser operation requires careful control of the pump intensity distribution along the laser medium. Any deviation from this distribution will result to heating or cooling in some parts of the laser medium, which can be estimated with Equation (9). Since $i_P(z) > 0$, one can see in Equation (14) that there is a minimum value of laser signal intensity in the laser cavity that can undergo athermal amplification:

$$I_L^{min} = \frac{\hbar \omega_l \sigma_p^a}{\tau_R \left(\sigma_a^P \sigma_e^L - \sigma_a^L \sigma_e^P\right)} \left(\frac{\omega_F - \omega_P}{\omega_P - \omega_L}\right) \tag{15}$$

A comprehensive theory of the radiation-balanced (athermal) RE-doped bulk solid-state laser was developed in [14]. In [26], it was enhanced for the radiation-balanced (athermal) RE-doped fibre amplifiers.

3.2.2. Athermal Lasing in Real Systems

In the above section, perfect laser materials were considered, which are free from background absorption and are optically thin. Let us consider more realistic laser systems taking into account quenching, radiative trapping, and background absorption. These effects are present in all laser systems. Quenching of the laser excitation could occur through electron–phonon deactivation and through ion–ion energy transfer [27]. As a result, the radiative lifetime of an RE ion, τ_R, must be replaced by a fluorescence lifetime, τ_F. Energy transfer losses can be arranged with a characteristic quenching lifetime, τ_Q [27]. Radiation trapping occurs as a result of fluorescence reabsorption and its reflection from the sample boundaries. It can complicate the modeling of the laser systems. Radiation trapping can be taken into account with the effective values for mean fluorescence wavelength, $\tilde{\lambda}_F$, and lifetimes $\tilde{\tau}_F$, $\tilde{\tau}_Q$. These values can be obtained experimentally. For example, for an optically thin Yb^{3+}:KGW sample with the Yb^{3+} ion concentration $N_T = 2.2 \times 10^{20}$ cm^{-3} the mean fluorescence wavelength and the fluorescence lifetime are $\lambda_F = 997$ nm and $\tau_F = 0.275$ ms, respectively. For the 2 mm × 8 mm, Yb^{3+}:KGW sample fluorescent trapping increases these values to $\tilde{\lambda}_F = 1011$ nm and $\tilde{\tau}_F = 0.75$ ms. The rate equation for the radiation trapped system has the form

$$\frac{dN_2}{dt} = \frac{I_P}{\hbar \omega_P}\left(N_T \sigma_a^P - N_2\left(\sigma_a^P + \sigma_e^P\right)\right) + \frac{I_L}{\hbar \omega_L}\left(N_T \sigma_a^L - N_2\left(\sigma_a^L + \sigma_e^L\right)\right) - \frac{N_2}{\tilde{\tau}_F} - \frac{N_2^2}{N_T \tilde{\tau}_Q} \tag{16}$$

It must be used to simulate heat generated with the quantum defect. Unavoidable impurities in the laser host material result in background absorption, which can be described by the background absorption coefficient $\alpha_B(\lambda)$. Even small background absorption can significantly deteriorate the laser cooling process. The heat power density generated in the laser by quenching can be described as

$$P_{heat}^Q = \hbar \omega_P N_T \tilde{N}_2 \left(\frac{1}{\tau_F} - \frac{1}{\tau_R} + \frac{\tilde{N}_2}{\tilde{\tau}_Q}\right), \tag{17}$$

where

$$\tilde{N}_2 \approx \frac{N_2}{N_T}\left(1 + \frac{(1 - \tau_R/\tilde{\tau}_F) - N_2 \tau_R/(N_T \tilde{\tau}_Q)}{\tilde{I}_P + \tilde{I}_L + \tau_R/\tilde{\tau}_F}\right), \tag{18}$$

and

$$\tilde{I}_{P,L} = I_{P,L} \frac{\tau_R\left(\sigma_a^{P,L} + \sigma_e^{P,L}\right)}{\hbar \omega_{P,L}}. \tag{19}$$

The heat power density caused by background absorption has the form

$$P_{heat}^a = \frac{\hbar}{\tau_R}\left(\frac{\tilde{i}_P \omega_P \alpha_B(\lambda_P)}{\sigma_a^P + \sigma_e^P} + \frac{\tilde{i}_L \omega_L \alpha_B(\lambda_L)}{\sigma_a^L + \sigma_e^L}\right), \tag{20}$$

where $\tilde{i}_{P,L} = I_{P,L}/\tilde{I}_{P,L}$. These values must be added to the heat power density generated with the quantum defect if one wants to simulate the heat power density generated by different effects in the realistic laser system.

Summarizing the theory of radiation-balanced lasing, it is important to emphasize that laser materials suitable to radiation-balanced lasing must have two widely separated sets of discreet energy levels (manifolds) such that nonradiative transitions between them are unlikely. They also must have negligible background absorption. A properly arranged reliable pump system, the shape of a laser gain medium, and material selection criteria can result in little or no heat generation within solid-state lasers.

4. Development of Radiation-Balanced Lasers

The thermodynamics of radiation-balanced lasers has been discussed both qualitatively and quantitatively from the point of view of the first and second laws by Mungan [28] The Carnot efficiency has been derived for optical amplification from consideration of the radiative transport of energy and entropy. It has been shown that the highest Carnot efficiencies can be reached only when the system is pumped into saturation. Indeed, the energy of a collection of photons of fixed mean frequency and angular divergence scales linearly with the number of photons. The entropy of the set depends on the number and on the energy distribution of the photons. As the number of photons in the pump beam increases, the entropy that the beam carries per photon decreases since it becomes more sharply peaked. As the fluorescence intensity increases, the entropy decreases, but it does not decrease as rapidly as does the pump beam, because the spontaneously emitted light is less intense, broader in bandwidth, and distributed over a larger range of solid angles than is the pump radiation.

As one can see from the theory developed in the previous part of the paper, a detailed balance of the stimulated and spontaneous emission at each point of the laser medium can provide a solid-state laser that generates no internal heat. Unfortunately, there are two serious problems associated with the practical development of radiation-balanced amplifiers and lasers: the precise control of the pump power and almost linear growth of the amplified signal (Figure 5). The linear growth of the power of the amplified signal requires an enormous increase in the length of the active medium for very high output power. The athermal bulk or fibre laser requires precision control of the pump power at each point along the length laser medium. This is not a simple problem, especially in the case of a fibre amplifier or laser. The sensitivity and stability of a radiation-balanced laser to perturbations in the field parameters and temperature have been analyzed in [29]. As one can see in [29], fluctuations in the gain set limits on the variability of the pump wavelength. A pump stability of ±1 nm was suggested for an Yb:KGW laser. An active wavelength stabilization scheme based on techniques for spatial mode matching was presented in [29]. A dynamic control to the laser system based on the pump wavelength shift was proposed. It permits to minimize the sensitivity of the athermal laser to ambient temperature fluctuations. The idea to use tapered reflectance mirrors to flatten the transverse laser profile and to improve optical efficiency was considered in [29].

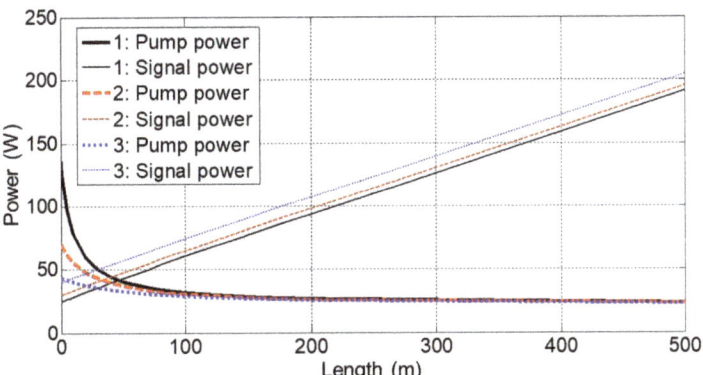

Figure 5. Dependence of the signal and pump powers from the length of the athermal fibre amplifier for three different input signal powers: (1) 25 W, (2) 30 W, and (3) 40 W [26].

4.1. Athermal Bulk Lasers

Since the first experimental observation in 1995, laser cooling of solids has been realized with Yb^{3+}, Er^{3+}, Tm^{3+}, and Ho^{3+} ions doped in a wide variety of low phonon glasses and crystals. Yb^{3+} ions are the most promising RE ions for laser cooling applications. They have only one excited manifold, so that Yb^{3+} ions are free from excited state absorption, which can be a source of multi-phonon decay resulting in undesirable heat generation in the system.

Experiments devoted to radiation-balanced lasers began at the Naval Research Laboratory (NRL) in 1999 [30]. New materials for laser cooling were investigated. In 2002, the first athermal bulk laser was experimentally demonstrated with an Yb^{3+}:$KGd(WO_4)_2$ crystal [31]. The laser design based on direct diode pumping of Yb^{3+}:$KGd(WO_4)_2$ crystals was developed further in [32].

Successful laser systems are based on high-quality materials. YAG and fused silica are the best choice. They have the highest optical quality and lowest losses. In 2010, the Yb^{3+}:YAG laser rods with Yb^{3+} concentrations of 1%, 2%, 3%, and 5% were investigated.

The scheme of the radiation-balanced laser based on the Yb^{3+}:YAG laser rod is presented in Figure 6. High power pumping with fibre lasers at 1030 nm produced a near diffraction limited laser at 1050 nm. The mean fluorescent wavelength for Yb^{3+}:YAG is 1010 nm. Lower thermal loading and better beam quality were reached with the 2% Yb^{3+}:YAG rod. The average power of up to 200 W of output with a beam quality of $M^2 = 1.2$ was demonstrated without significant thermal loading or thermo-optic distortions [33]. A typical thermal image of the Yb^{3+}:YAG rod inside the athermal laser is presented in Figure 7. Thermal loads were reduced to below 0.01% relative to the laser output power. As one can see in Figure 7, fluorescence for the laser rod heats the mirror on the left. The thermally insulated laser rod is almost not heated. Its temperature is very close to the ambient temperature.

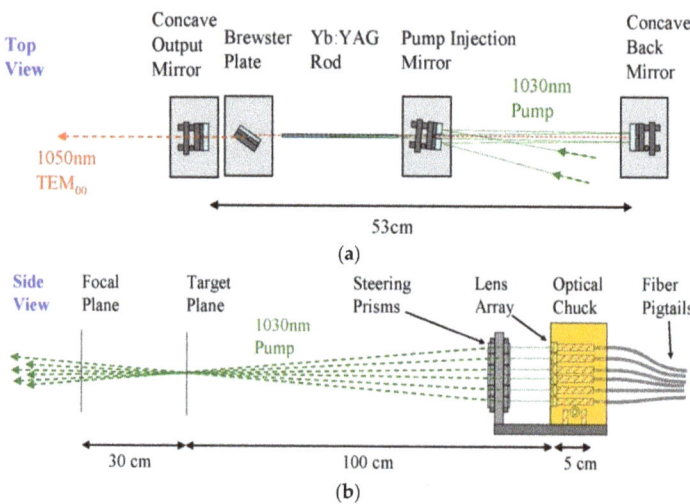

Figure 6. Athermal laser: (**a**) Stable Yb^{3+}:YAG resonator. (**b**) Ytterbium fibre laser pump array propagation shown without the target laser rod [34].

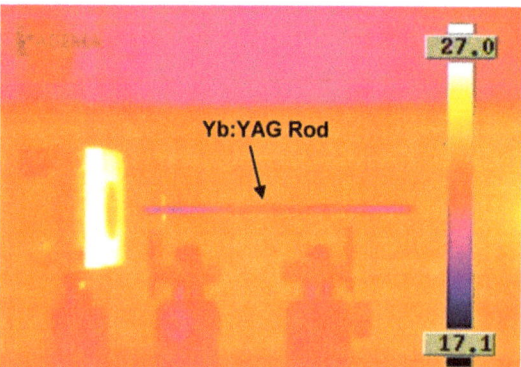

Figure 7. Yb^{3+}:YAG rod inside the laser. This image was captured after 10 s of lasing at 70 W with an ambient temperature of 22 °C. The color scale corresponds to ∓5 °C as shown on right. Fluorescence from the laser rod heats the mount for the pump injection mirror on left [33].

To improve laser performance, the laser rod was replaced with a slab composed of Yb^{3+}:YAG and sapphire (Figure 8) [34]. As one can see in Figure 8, a single 2 mm × 110 mm 3% Yb^{3+}:YAG sample was fusion-bonded to a sapphire plate along its length. The sapphire plate provides a refractive index mismatch of 0.07, significantly reducing fluorescence trapping and providing guiding of the pump at the wavelength 1030 nm. The sapphire bond permitted to reduce the fluorescence lifetime from 2 ms to 1.25 ms. Using this laser design, 1 W of heat for every kilowatt of output laser power was realized.

4.2. Athermal Disk Lasers

In 2000, an Yb^{3+}:KGW laser disk was edge-pumped with radially focused laser diode bars (Figure 9a) [34]. It generated up to 490 W. This was the first system with heat loading below the laser quantum defect.

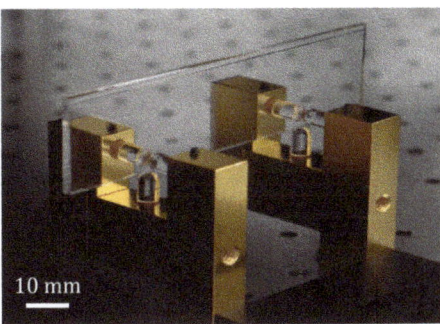

Figure 8. Radiation-balanced laser gain element constructed from a tapered 110 mm 3% Yb^{3+}:YAG slab fusion-bonded to a 2 mm × 20 mm sapphire plate. The sapphire plate provides a refractive index mismatch of 0.07. This allows for guiding of the 1030 nm pump lasers while significantly reducing fluorescent trapping. The gold-plated mount and fused silica pins were designed to avoid radiative heating of the fixture [34].

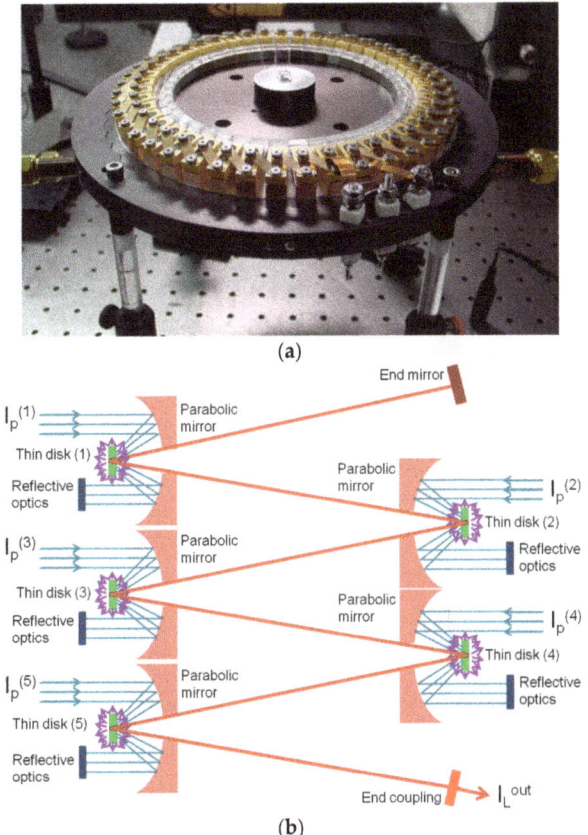

Figure 9. Yb^{3+}:KGW disk lasers. (**a**) Edge-pumped Yb^{3+}:KGW disk laser with a laser quantum defect of 4.8%. (**b**) Thin-disk athermal laser system. $I_p^{(1)}$, $I_p^{(2)}$, $I_p^{(3)}$, $I_p^{(4)}$, and $I_p^{(5)}$ are the pump intensities, I_L^{out} is the intensity of the output laser signal. The violet arrows around the disks illustrate anti-Stokes fluorescence [35].

In 2014, a thin-disk athermal laser system was proposed and theoretically analysed [35]. This scheme, consisting of a sequence of thin disks, can provide high flexibility, which is key for athermal laser operation (Figure 9b). Yb^{3+}:KGW laser disks were considered in [35]. The sequence of thin disks provides precise control of the pump intensity on each disk. It allows the control of the pump intensity almost locally; that is, almost at each point along all laser gain medium. In addition, the generic design of the laser module allows easy scaling to higher powers. The concentration of the ions, as well as the thickness, can be changed from one disk to another.

In 2019, the radiation-balanced Yb^{3+}:YAG disk laser was experimentally demonstrated in an intracavity pumping geometry (Figure 10) [36]. An optically pumped vertical-external-cavity surface-emitting laser (VECSEL) was used to enhance the pump absorption. The broad tunability and good beam quality of VECSELs provided additional parametrical freedom (Figure 10).

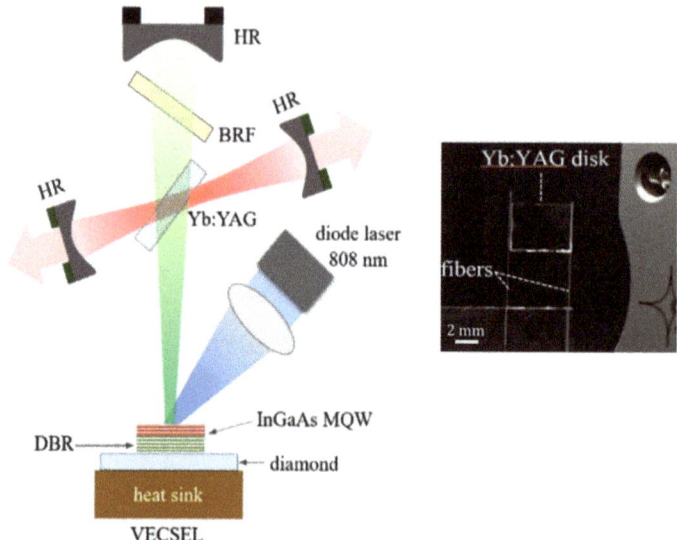

Figure 10. Schematic of the intracavity-pumped radiation-balanced disk laser setup. On the right, the mounting of the 5%-doped Yb^{3+}:YAG disk of 0.5 mm thick and 4 mm × 5 mm cross section is shown where it is glued onto two bare fibres, which are in turn supported by a glass slide to reduce the heat load [36].

The thermal images of the mounted laser disk at room temperature after 30 min at radiation-balanced condition are presented in Figure 11. Darker shades represent lower temperatures. Recorded thermal images of the unpumped laser disk at room temperatures, and under pump, are shown in Figures 11a and 11b, respectively. Figure 11c illustrates the temperature dynamics of the radiation-balanced process. The temperature profile of the laser disk was monitored with a thermal camera (Nanocore 640, L3 Communications Corporation, Garland, TX, USA) with 0.05 K resolution as the VECSEL power was varied. As one can see in Figure 11c, net cooling takes place from the very beginning, that is, as soon as the pump diode is turned on. Indeed, the VECSEL and the fluorescence emission process start immediately. The lasing process with the Yb^{3+}:YAG disk takes some time to initiate. It warms up the laser disk. About 10% power fluctuation was observed in the first 5 min of the experiment. The radiation balancing condition was realized with 57 W of incident pump power at 808 nm, or 32 W of absorbed power. About 1 W output power radiation balance was obtained. A temperature difference of ~2 K was observed between the centre and the edge of the disk of 4 mm × 5 mm cross section as a result of

Gaussian radial intensity distribution of the modes. Beam shaping can be used to mitigate this temperature difference.

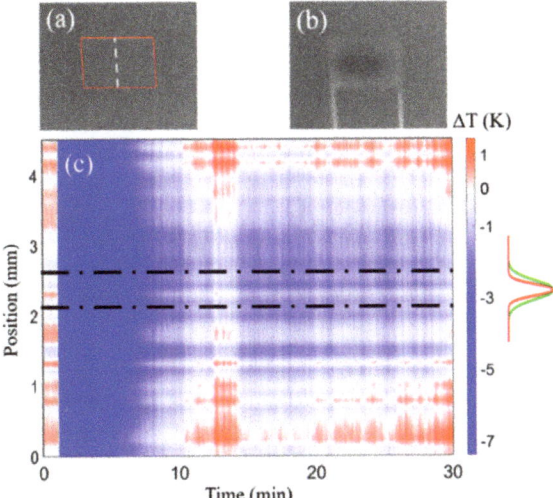

Figure 11. The thermal images of the laser disk; (**a**) is the unpumped laser disk at room temperature. The red lines represent the outline of the disk; (**b**) is the laser pumped disk. (**c**) The line-integrated time-evolution of the temperature change along the white dashed line in (**a**). The VECSEL cavity is unblocked at 1 min [36].

Recently, Yb^{3+}:YLF and Yb^{3+}:LLF laser disks have been investigated in external multipass pumping schemes (Figure 12) [37,38]. Compared to intracavity pumping, external multipass pumping offers higher control on pump spot size and mode-matching conditions. LLF is an isomorph of YLF. They have very similar thermo-optics properties. The Yb^{3+}:YLF and Yb^{3+}:LLF laser disks with the Yb^{3+} concentration of 10%, 1 mm thick, and 5 mm diameter were pumped at the wavelength 1020 nm corresponding to the lowest energy transition between ground and excited manifolds of Yb^{3+} ions. This wavelength is convenient for the system cooling. Laser emission was observed around 1050 nm. The linear laser cavity is constituted by mirrors M1 and M3, both with 10 cm radius of curvature (Figure 12a). A hole in the center of the M2 mirror allows propagation of the laser mode. The input laser beam was focused near the focal point of M1 and M2, and thus collimated after reflection of M2 and focused again after reflection on M1. A tilted window at Brewster's angle was used to shift the beam towards the center of M2. After several roundtrips between M1 and M2, the pump is eventually scattered out by the sidewalls of the window. The sample was placed at the middle point of M1 and M2. Radiation-balanced operation at about 1 W output power was achieved with the Yb^{3+}:YLF disk. Radiation-balanced laser operation was observed at about 200 mW output power with the Yb^{3+}:LLF laser disk (Figure 12b). It was shown that large transversal thermal gradients are expected in beam area for high-power (kW) radiation-balanced laser operations that require mitigation techniques.

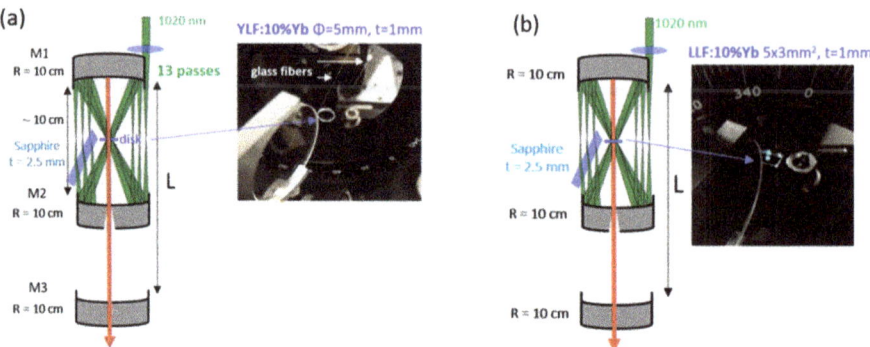

Figure 12. Schematic of laser cavity and multipass pumping for (**a**) the Yb^{3+}:YLF laser disk and for (**b**) the Yb^{3+}:LLF laser disk [38].

4.3. Athermal Fibre Lasers

As previously noted, in radiation-balanced lasers and amplifiers, the radiated energy increases only linearly with the length of the active medium. This requires a long active medium, which is undesirable. To overcome the problem, lasers and amplifiers with a cooler made from RE ions and integrated in the body of the device have been proposed and theoretically investigated by Nemova and Kashyap [39–41].

As one can see in Figure 13a, the properly distributed Yb^{3+} ions pumped at the wavelength 1015 nm with a cooling pump power P_p^{cool} work as an integrated cooler, compensating for the heat generated inside the active medium due to the quantum defect in the Raman lasers or amplifiers. In this scheme, the lasing action is separated from the cooling process. Such separation of actions provides flexibility in the laser design. It permits one to maintain the exponential growth of the amplified signal along the length of the laser medium.

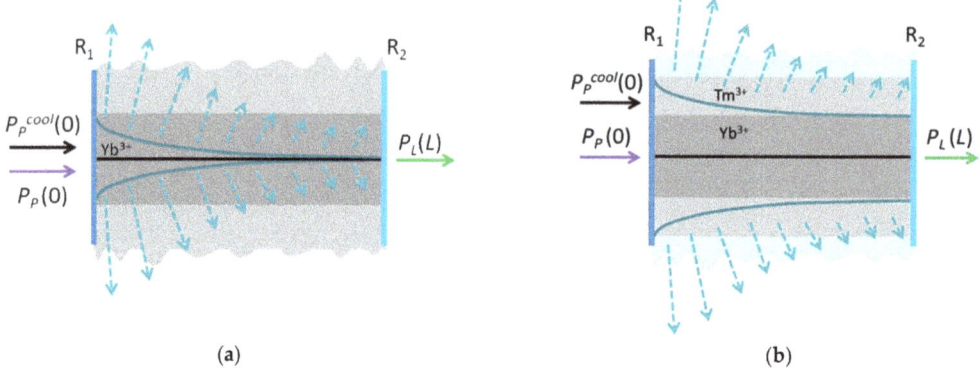

Figure 13. Fibre lasers with an integrated cooler. (**a**) Athermal Raman fibre laser. Two curves in the core illustrate the distribution of Yb^{3+} ions providing cooling. (**b**) Athermal Yb^{3+}-doped fibre laser with the Tm^{3+}-doped cladding. Two curves in the cladding illustrate the distribution of Tm^{3+} ions providing cooling. The dashed arrows illustrate anti-Stokes fluorescence [41].

Figure 13b illustrates an athermal Yb^{3+}-doped fibre laser, in which the heating is caused by Stokes-shifted stimulated emission generated during the lasing process. In this scheme, the lasing process takes place in the Yb^{3+}-doped fibre core. The cooling process takes place in the Tm^{3+}-doped fibre cladding pumped at a wavelength of 1900 nm, that is, in the long-wavelength tail of the Tm^{3+} absorption spectrum. Here, the Tm^{3+} ions play the role of an integrated cooler. The distribution of the RE ions in the integrated cooler is properly arranged in both schemes to provide complete compensation for the heat in the case of fixed laser pump power, P_p. The dashed arrows in Figure 13 illustrate anti-Stokes fluorescence. A deviation in the laser input pump power causes a small deviation in complete compensation of the temperature along the length of the laser medium. However, this deviation in the temperature is small in comparison with the peak temperature change without cooling. It can be partially compensated for by a change in the cooling pump power, P_p^{cool}.

The temperature distribution inside a double-cladding optical fibre laser or amplifier was theoretically investigated by Mafi [42]. It has been shown that heat generation in the cladding due to the parasitic absorption of the high-power pump must be taken into account in modern high-power fibre lasers and amplifiers, where the quantum defect is lowered, or when the amplifier operates in a nearly radiation-balanced regime, or for radiation-balanced lasers. The developed approach permits one to interpolate between the case where the quantum defect heating is dominant and when the parasitic absorption heating is comparable in size or is the dominant source of heating.

4.3.1. Athermal ZBLAN Fibre Lasers

An ytterbium-doped ZrF4–BaF2–LaF3–AlF3–NaF (ZBLAN) optical fibre was experimentally investigated to extract its laser cooling related parameters [43]. It has been shown that the Yb^{3+}:ZBLAN fibre is a viable laser-cooling medium for radiation-balanced lasers and amplifiers. A comparison between a conventional Yb^{3+}:ZBLAN fibre laser pumped at 975 nm wavelength and an athermal Yb^{3+}:ZBLAN fibre laser pumped at 1030 nm was made [43]. They are presented in Figure 14. The output laser signal in both lasers was assumed to be 3 W in power at the wavelength 1070 nm. Both systems were optimized for maximum efficiency. As one can see in Figure 14, the temperature rise in both designs is comparable, while the athermal laser required a 20-fold larger pump power, making the athermal laser design totally unpractical. The authors of [43] attributed the problem to the relatively large value of the background absorption of the pump. They considered the problem of the background absorption in [44]. Following their simulations, a 10-fold reduction in the background absorption can reduce the heating in the athermal laser design significantly, rendering the athermal laser viable. These results are presented in Figure 14.

In 2021, the first observation of anti-Stokes cooling of Yb^{3+}:ZBLAN fibres, in which both the core and the cladding were doped with Yb^{3+} to increase the number of Yb^{3+} ions contributing to cooling, was announced [45]. It is worth mentioning that laser cooling of the core-doped Yb^{3+}:ZBLAN fibres was demonstrated previously in a vacuum [46] and at atmospheric pressure [47,48]. The main goal of [45] was to provide an experimental validation of the concept of cooling a fibre more aggressively by doping its cladding with a cooling ion and pumping the cladding, which was proposed by Nemova and Kashyap in [39]. The performances of three fibre designs were compared. One of these fibres was a conventional large-core multimode fibre. Two others were cladding-doped fibres. One of these two cladding-doped fibres had a double-D shape, and the other had an octagonal cladding. Both shapes were designed to induce greater mode mixing (Figure 15). The pump light from a 1025.5 nm fibre-pigtailed semiconductor laser was launched into the Yb^{3+}:ZBLAN fibre under test. The temperature change of a fibre was measured with a custom slow-light FBG sensor with a sub-mK resolution [49].

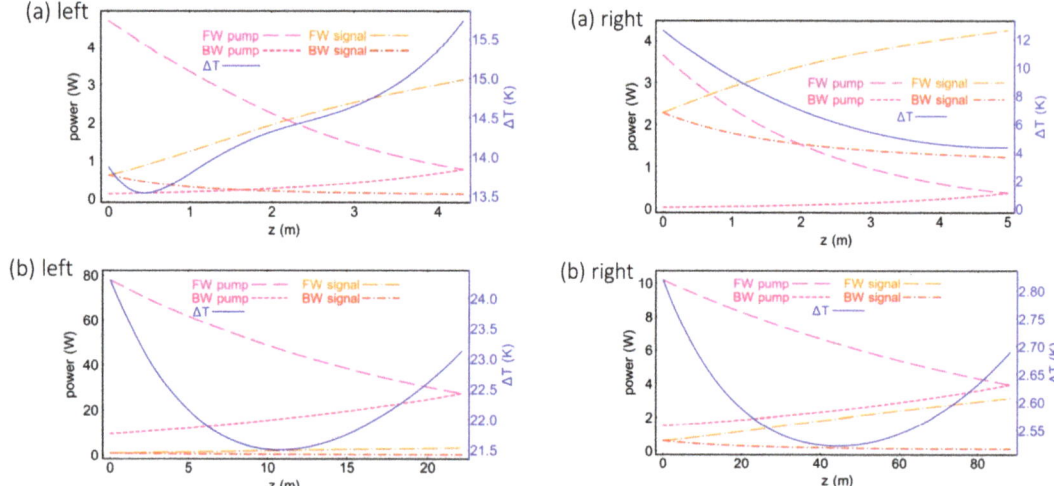

Figure 14. (a) Propagation of the forward pump (FW pump), backward pump (BW pump), forward signal (FW signal), backward signal (BW signal), and temperature rise along the fibre for a conventional fibre laser pumped at 975 nm. (b) Similar graph for the athermal laser operation pumped at 1030 nm. In (a,b) on the left, the background absorption is 4.278×10^{-2} m^{-1}. In (a,b) on the right, a 10-fold reduction is shown in the background absorption [43,44].

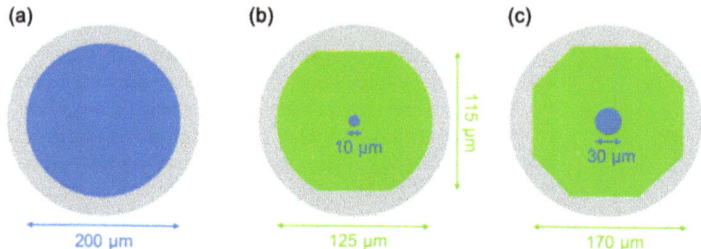

Figure 15. Cross section of the multimode Yb-doped ZBLAN fibres used in [45]: (a) conventional multimode fibre, (b) double-D cladding-doped fibre, and (c) cladding-doped fibre with an octagonal inner cladding [45].

The conventional multimode fibre (Figure 15a) with relatively poor mode mixing due to its symmetrical core was used to illustrate the importance of mode mixing. The maximum measured temperature change observed in this fibre under 1025.5 nm pumping was −0.65 K for 584 mW of pump power at the location of the sensor.

In order to improve mode mixing, a second fibre with a double-D cladding doped with Yb^{3+} was fabricated (Figure 15b). The largest temperature change recorded for this fibre was −78 mK for a pump power of 240 mW. The efficiency (temperature change divided by pump power) was higher (~3 times) than in the conventional multimode fibre.

The third Yb^{3+}:ZBLAN fibre, which had an octagonal cladding, was designed specifically to improve the mode filling of the cladding (Figure 15c). This fibre design permits the mode to fill a noticeably larger portion of the cladding. The temperature change of −1.3 K was reached with the maximum available pump power of 3 W. To improve this value, the fibre was pumped with the pump power of 15 W at the wavelength 1040 nm. The temperature change of −2 K was reached.

The fibre with a double-D cladding (Figure 15b) did not perform as well as the fibre with an octagonal inner cladding (Figure 15c), largely due to limited mode mixing, which resulted in only a small fraction of the ions in the cladding being excited and contributing to the refrigeration process. An octagonal inner cladding of the fibre (Figure 15c) permitted to increase mode mixing and excite the cladding more uniformly. As a result, greater cooling was observed with this fibre.

4.3.2. Athermal Silica Fibre Lasers

Most commercial fibre lasers are made of silica, due to silica's low loss and durability. Laser powers as high as 10 kW have been achieved with a silica fibre laser [50]. However, crystals and fluoride-based samples are widely used hosts for laser cooling with anti-Stokes fluorescence. Relative to silica, fluorides have fairly high loss and brittleness, that is, they can undergo sudden structural failure instead of plastic deformation. As a result, the highest power achieved with a ZBLAN laser is only 50 W [51].

In 2019, laser cooling with anti-Stokes fluorescence was demonstrated in two separate silica samples: a silica fibre [52] and a bulk silica preform [53]. These results were breakthroughs for development of silica-based athermal lasers. In [54], several influential factors on laser cooling with anti-Stokes fluorescence in silica fibres were investigated. The cooling performances of six Yb^{3+}-doped silica fibres with various dopant and codopant concentrations, OH^- loss, and core dimensions were compared. It was shown that silica can accommodate unexpectedly high Yb^{3+} concentrations without suffering from quenching, in spite of its high phonon energy. Cooling a fibre with high 2.52 wt.% Yb^{3+} concentration was enabled by reducing the absorptive loss below 5 dB/km and codoping the fibre with 2.0 wt.% Al, leading to a record-breaking critical quenching concentration, 30% higher than the previous reported. A temperature change of −70 mK was observed at atmospheric pressure for 170 mW/m of pump power absorbed at 1040 nm.

In 2021, the first radiation-balanced silica fibre amplifier was demonstrated. An Yb^{3+}-doped silica fibre served as an active medium [55]. The core diameter of the silica fibre was 21 µm. Its numerical aperture was 0.13. The Yb^{3+} concentration was 2.52 wt.%. The fibre was codoped with 2.00 wt.% Al to reduce concentration quenching. The wavelength of the pump was 1040 nm and the signal wavelength was 1064 nm. The mean fluorescence wavelength of Yb^{3+} was 1003.9 nm and the radiative and quenching lifetimes were 765 µs and 38 ms, respectively. The Yb^{3+} critical quenching concentration was 21.0 wt.%. The absorptive loss of the fibre was 18 dB/km. The temporal trace of the temperature change in this fibre amplifier is illustrated in Figure 16. At time $t = 0$ s, the pump was turned on. The temperature of the fibre decreased ∼130 mK below room temperature. After 15 s, the seed signal was turned on. The temperature of the fibre increased, reaching a new steady-state value of ∼110 mK below room temperature. The temperature change of the fibre amplifier was defined as the difference between the average temperature in the first 5 s, when both the pump and signal were off, and the average temperature in the last 5 s after both had been turned on. Each measurement was repeated three times and averaged. Measured temperature change versus position along the fibre amplifier is presented in Figure 17. The solid curves in Figure 17 are simulation results obtained using the model of a radiation-balanced fibre laser described in [56]. In [55], it was shown that light can be coherently amplified with a gain approaching 20 dB and generating no net internal heating.

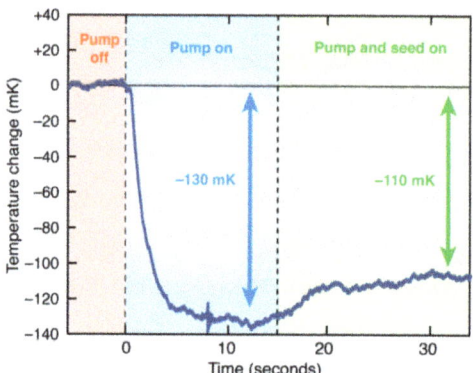

Figure 16. Measured temporal trace of the temperature change in the Yb^{3+}-doped silica fibre as the 1040 nm pump and 1064 nm seed are sequentially turned on, launching 1.64 W and 3 mW in the fibre core, respectively [55].

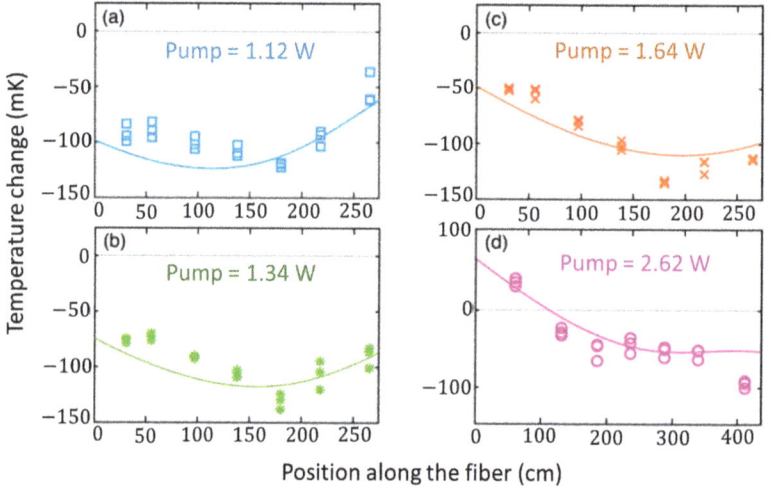

Figure 17. Measured temperature change versus position along the fibre amplifier, and simulated dependencies using the model based on [55]: for (a–c) a 2.74 m, and (d) a 4.35 m amplifier fibre [55].

4.3.3. Athermal Fibre Lasers with Optically Active Composite Cladding Materials

The idea to use composite materials, such as glass–ceramic, for laser cooling with anti-Stokes fluorescence was proposed by Nemova and Kashyap in 2012 [57,58]. They proposed to use Tm^{3+}-doped oxy-fluoride glass–ceramic to combine the low phonon energy of the Tm^{3+} doped fluoride nanocrystals with the promising mechanical and chemical properties of the oxide glass. In such a structure, Tm^{3+}-doped nanocrystals serve as optically active sources of cooling.

Recently, the idea to use composite materials for optical cooling was experimentally developed and applied to fibre lasers by Xia et al. [59,60]. As a proof of principle, they demonstrated laser cooling of an YLF/polymer composite cladding material using far-field excitation [60]. As one can see in Figure 18a, a cladding-etched bare glass fibre with YLF crystals attached to it using a layer of commercially available fluoropolymer CYTOP with an ultra-low NIR absorption coefficient was illuminated perpendicularly in the far field with a 1020 nm continuous wave laser focused onto a crystal at a range of irradiances up to 1 MW/cm^2. The pump laser at the wavelength 1020 nm excites electrons from energy level E_4 to energy level E_5. After thermalization accompanied by phonon absorption in the $^3F_{5/2}$ manifold, electrons undergo transition to the $^3F_{7/2}$ manifold, and the fluorescence spectrum arises (Figure 18b). The fluorescence spectra were recorded with a spectrometer (Ocean Optics, NIR512, Midland, ON, Canada). A 1000 nm short-pass filter (Thorlabs, FESH1000, Newton, MA, USA) was used to filter the laser line. Ten spectra, collected for 100 ms each, were averaged to obtain the final fluorescence spectrum. The temperature-calibrated fluorescence spectra were obtained using a cryostat (Janis, ST500, Westerville, OH, USA) in which the sample temperature was maintained at various points from 300 K to 350 K by a temperature controller (Lake Shore, 335, Westerville, OH, USA) with resolution 0.01 K. Fluorescence spectra were normalized to the peak at 960 nm. P1 and P2 are electronic transitions E6−E2 and E5−E2/E3, respectively. The integrated intensity ratio of P1 and P2 peaks is temperature dependent following a Boltzmann distribution (Figure 18c). The integration ranges for P1 and P2 are from 952 nm to 968 nm and from 986 nm to 1000 nm, respectively. It was shown that the temperature of the Yb^{3+}:YLF crystal decreases by 6.6 K (Figure 18c). At each laser irradiance, a mean P1/P2 ratio was obtained by averaging six measurements, and the error bars represent one standard deviation, which are smaller than 1% of the mean values.

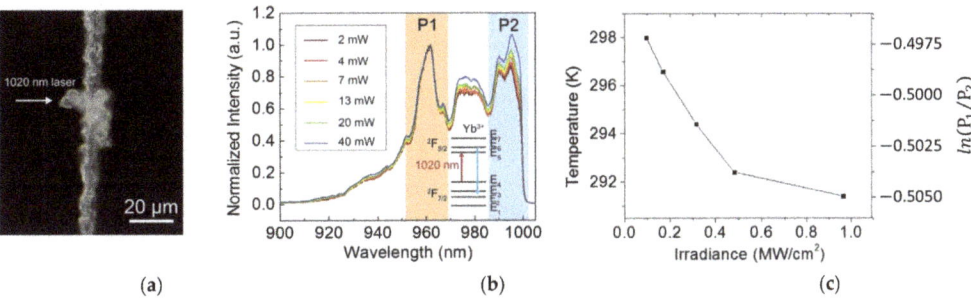

Figure 18. (a) Optical microscope image of Yb^{3+}:YLF microcrystals on an etched fibre. (b) Yb^{3+}:YLF fluorescence spectra at various laser irradiances, normalized to the P1 peak. At higher irradiance the P2 peak increases in intensity. (c) The integrated intensity ratio of P1 and P2 peaks with the corresponding calibrated temperature at each laser irradiance [60].

In [60], Xia et al. proposed and theoretically analyzed the fibre laser with two claddings (Figure 19). One of these claddings (the inner one) is composed of glass with Yb^{3+}:YLF nanocrystals. It covers the Yb^{3+}-doped fibre glass core. The outer cladding is made of the same glass as the inner cladding, but without Yb^{3+}:YLF nanocrystals. The authors of this paper expect that the optically pumped Yb^{3+}:YLF nanocrystals in the inner cladding will lower the local temperature through anti-Stokes fluorescence. They proposed to reduce Rayleigh scattering by index matching the composite host material with the index of YLF. Their model shows a significant temperature decrease of 19 K when the Yb^{3+}:YLF nanocrystals within the composite cladding have a volume fraction of 10%.

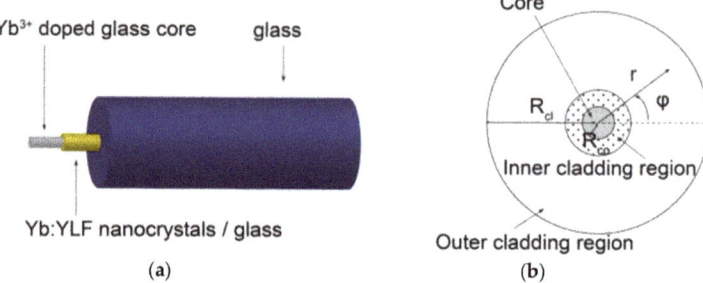

Figure 19. (a) The core of the fibre is Yb^{3+}-doped glass. The inner region of the cladding (yellow) is composed of glass and YLF nanocrystals, and the outer region of the cladding (blue) is made of the same glass as the inner cladding region, but with no Yb^{3+}:YLF. (b) The fibre cross section [60].

4.4. Athermal Spherical Microlasers

Microlasers fabricated from upconverting nanoparticles (UCNP) coupled to whispering gallery mode (WGM) microresonators were demonstrated in [61,62]. They can exhibit continuous wave anti-Stokes lasing useful for tracking cells, environmental sensing, and coherent stimulation of biological activity. Continuous-wave anti-Stokes lasing with laser thresholds as low as 1.7 ± 0.7 kW/cm^2 was achieved.

The radiation-balanced version of the spherical microlaser was proposed in [63]. As one can see in Figure 20a, in this athermal microlaser the monolayer of UCNPs is deposited on the surface of the microsphere. This monolayer consists of two different UCNPs: Yb^{3+}-doped β-NaYF4 UCNPs, which are responsible for optical refrigeration, and $Yb^{3+}/Er^{3+}/Tm^{3+}$-codoped β-NaYF4 UCNPs, which serve as solid-state gain media. In this scheme, the cooling power and the stimulated emission are provided by UCNPs with different compositions operating at the same pump wavelength.

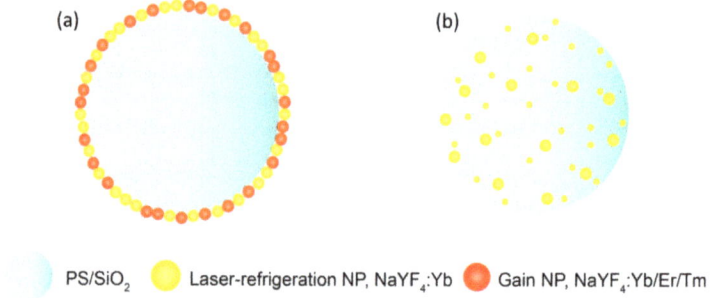

Figure 20. Schematics of (**a**) a radiation-balanced microlaser and (**b**) a 3D composite laser refrigeration microsphere [63].

The authors of [63] also proposed to use Yb^{3+}-doped UCNPs distributed throughout the entire volume of the microsphere for its optical cooling (Figure 20b). The athermal operation of microsphere lasers has not been demonstrated yet.

5. Conclusions

The presented work gives an overview of the latest achievements in a very promising and intensively developing area of laser physics known as radiation-balanced or athermal lasers. It is shown that the radiation balance can be maintained using optical refrigeration based on anti-Stokes fluorescence in the system of RE ions doped in a low-phonon host material. Optical refrigeration is the only solid-state technology that can cool to cryogenic temperatures. A basic model describing the operation of radiation-balanced lasers has been presented and discussed. The analytic expressions describing radiation-balanced laser operation were obtained using the set of coupled rate equations. The requirements for radiation balance predict that the characteristics of a radiation-balanced laser are affected by cavity parameters and fundamental material properties. The pump wavelength is the most sensitive parameter. To attain optical refrigeration in the laser, the pump wavelength must exceed the mean fluorescence wavelength.

At the present time, athermal lasers follow four main designs: radiation-balanced bulk and fibre lasers, radiation-balanced disk lasers, and athermal microlasers. All four designs considered in this review are very promising for different applications. Anti-Stokes cooling of RE-doped bulk, fibre, and disk lasers have been experimentally demonstrated. Both experiments and calculations indicate that improving the purity of host crystals will result into improving athermal laser performance. The development of new RE-doped low-phonon materials can facilitate the realization of athermal lasers and accelerate their commercialisation. Recently, Nakayama et al. [64,65] proposed to use Yb^{3+}-doped yttrium aluminum perovskite (YAP) as an active medium of radiation-balanced lasers. YAP has properties that are similar to those of YAG, but it possesses a phonon energy (620 cm^{-1}) that is lower than that of YAG (865 cm^{-1}). This lower phonon energy is a source of higher quantum efficiency. It has been shown that the small-signal gain of athermal laser materials utilizing an $f - f$ transition of RE ions can be controlled by engineering the surrounding crystal fields of the RE dopant.

The further average power scaling requires better control of the beam intensity profile. Recently, athermal laser operation with mode-mismatched Gaussian and super-Gaussian beams was analyzed by Sheik-Bahae and Yang [66]. As one can see in [66], in a disk geometry, beam-area scaling to high-power operations can be accompanied by large transverse temperature gradients. These undesirable gradients can be countered by pump beam shaping and/or employing longer gain media.

Considering four main designs of radiation-balanced lasers, I believe that athermal disk lasers will be the first commercially available radiation-balanced lasers in the coming years. Indeed, the disk shape of a gain medium provides significant freedom in the control of pump power distribution, which is a key element for athermal operation of the laser.

Funding: This research received no external funding.

Institutional Review Board Statement: Not applicable.

Informed Consent Statement: Not applicable.

Data Availability Statement: Not applicable.

Acknowledgments: Not applicable.

Conflicts of Interest: The author declares no conflict of interest.

References

1. Keyes, R.J.; Quist, T.M. Injection luminescent pumping of CaF2:U^{3+} with GaAs diode lasers. *Appl. Phys. Lett.* **1964**, *4*, 50–52. [CrossRef]
2. Streifer, W.; Scifres, D.; Harnagel, G.; Welch, D.; Berger, J.; Sakamoto, M. Advances in laser diode pumps. *IEEE J. Quantum Electron.* **1988**, *24*, 883–894. [CrossRef]
3. Snitzer, E. Proposed fiber cavities for optical masers. *Appl. Phys.* **1964**, *32*, 36–39. [CrossRef]
4. Hegarty, J.; Broer, M.M.; Golding, B.; Simpson, J.R.; MacChesney, J.B. Photon echoes below 1 K in a Nd^{3+}- doped glass fiber. *Phys. Rev. Lett.* **1983**, *51*, 2033–2035. [CrossRef]
5. Poole, S.B.; Payne, D.N.; Fermann, M.E. Fabrication of low-loss optical fibers contalning rare-earth ions. *Electron. Lett.* **1985**, *21*, 737–738. [CrossRef]
6. Poole, S.B.; Payne, D.N.; Mears, R.J.; Fermann, M.E.; Laming, R.L. Fabrication and characterization of low loss optical fibers containing rare earth ions. *J. Lightwave Tech.* **1986**, *LT-4*, 870–876. [CrossRef]
7. Mears, R.J.; Reekie, L.; Poole, S.B.; Payne, D.N. Neodymium-doped silica single-miber lasers. *Electron. Lett.* **1985**, *21*, 737–738. [CrossRef]

8. Taverner, D.; Richardson, D.J.; Dong, L.; Caplen, J.E.; Williams, K.; Penty, R.V. 158-pJ pulses from a singletransverse-mode, large-mode-area erbium-doped fiber amplifier. *Opt. Lett.* **1997**, *22*, 378–380. [CrossRef]
9. Nemova, G.; Kashyap, R. High-power long period grating assisted EDFA. *J. Opt. Soc. Am. B* **2008**, *25*, 1322–1327. [CrossRef]
10. Martin, W.S.; Chernoch, J.P. Multiple Internal Reflection Face-Pumped Laser. U.S. Patent 3633126A, 4 January 1972.
11. Eggleston, J.M.; Frantz, L.M.; Injeyan, H. Derivation of the Frantz-Nodvik equation for zig-zag optical path, slab geometry laser amplifiers. *IEEE J. Qunntum Electron.* **1989**, *25*, 1855–1862. [CrossRef]
12. Giesen, A.; Hiigel, H.; Voss, A.; Wittig, K.; Brauch, U.; Opower, H. Scalable concept for diode-pumped high-power solid-state lasers. *Appl. Phys. B* **1994**, *58*, 365–372. [CrossRef]
13. Giesen, A.; Hugel, H.; Voss, A.; Wittig, K.; Brauch, U.; Opower, H. Diocle—Pumped high-power solid-state laser: Concept and first results with Yb:YAG. In *Advanced Solid State Lasers*; OSA Proceeding Series; Optical Society of America: Washington, DC, USA, 1994.
14. Bowman, S.R. Laser without internal heat generation. *IEEE J. Quantum Electron.* **1999**, *35*, 115–122. [CrossRef]
15. Nemova, G.; Kashyap, R. Laser cooling of solids. *Rep. Prog. Phys.* **2010**, *73*, 086501. [CrossRef]
16. Koechner, W. Absorbed pump power, thermal profile and stresses in a cw pumped Nd: YAG crystal. *Appl. Opt.* **1970**, *9*, 1429–1434. [CrossRef]
17. Schmid, M.; Graf, T.; Weber, H.P. Analytical model of the temperature distribution and the thermally induced birefringence in laser rods with cylindrically symmetric heating. *J. Opt. Soc. Am. B* **2000**, *17*, 1398–1404. [CrossRef]
18. Farrukh, U.; Buoncristiani, A.; Byvik, C. An analysis of the temperature distribution in finite solid-state laser rods. *IEEE J. Quantum Electron.* **1988**, *34*, 2253–2263. [CrossRef]
19. Innocenzi, M.; Yura, H.; Fincher, C.; Fields, R. Thermal modeling of continuous-wave end-pumped solidstate lasers. *Appl. Phys. Lett.* **1990**, *56*, 1831–1833. [CrossRef]
20. Chen, Y.; Huang, T.; Kao, C.; Wang, C.; Wang, S. Optimization in scaling fiber-coupled laser-diode endpumped lasers to higher power: Influence on thermal effect. *IEEE J. Quantum Electron.* **1997**, *33*, 1424–1429. [CrossRef]
21. Cousins, A. Temperature and thermal stress scaling in finite-length end-pumped laser rods. *IEEE J. Quantum Electron.* **1992**, *28*, 1057–1069. [CrossRef]
22. Pringsheim, P. Zwei Bemerkungen über den Unterschied von Lumineszenz- und Temperaturstrahlung. *Z. Phys.* **1929**, *57*, 739–746. [CrossRef]
23. Epstein, R.I.; Buchwald, M.I.; Edwards, B.C.; Gosnell, T.R.; Mungan, C.E. Observation of laser-induced fluorescent cooling of a solid. *Nat. Cell Biol.* **1995**, *377*, 500–502. [CrossRef]
24. Sheik-Bahae, M.; Epstein, R.I. Optical refrigeration. *Nat. Photonics* **2007**, *1*, 693–699. [CrossRef]
25. Andrianov, S.N.; Samartsev, V.V. Solid-state lasers with internal laser refrigeration effect. In Proceedings of the SPIE PECS'2001: Photon Echo and Coherent Spectroscopy, Nizhny Novgorod, Russia, 15 November 2001; Volume 4605, pp. 208–213.
26. Nemova, G.; Kashyap, R. Athermal continuous-wave fiber amplifier. *Opt. Commun.* **2009**, *282*, 2571–2575. [CrossRef]
27. Auzel, F. Upconversion and anti-Stokes processes with f and d ions in solids. *Chem. Rev.* **2004**, *104*, 139–173. [CrossRef]
28. Mungan, C.E. Thermodynamics of radiation-balanced lasing. *J. Opt. Soc. Am. B* **2003**, *20*, 1075–1082. [CrossRef]
29. Bowman, S.R.; Jenkins, N.W.; O'Connor, S.P.; Feldman, B.J. Sensitivity of stability of a radiation-balanced laser system. *IEEE J. Quantum Electron.* **2002**, *38*, 1339–1348. [CrossRef]
30. Bowman, S.R.; Mungan, C. New materials for optical cooling. *Appl. Phys. B* **2000**, *71*, 807–811. [CrossRef]
31. Bowman, S.R.; Jenkins, N.W.; Feldman, B.; O'Connor, S. Demonstration of a radiatively cooled laser. In Proceedings of the Conference on Lasers and Electro-Optics (CLEO), Long Beach, CA, USA, 24 May 2002.
32. Bowman, S.R.; O'Connor, S.; Biswal, S. Ytterbium laser with reduced thermal heating. *IEEE J. Quantum Electron.* **2005**, *41*, 1510–1517. [CrossRef]
33. Bowman, S.R.; O'Connor, S.P.; Biswal, S.; Condon, N.J.; Rosenberg, A. Minimizing heat generation in solid-state lasers. *IEEE J. Quantum Electron.* **2010**, *46*, 1076–1085. [CrossRef]
34. Bowman, S.R. Optically cooled lasers. In *Laser Cooling: Fundamental Properties and Application*; Nemova, G., Ed.; Pan Stanford Publishing Pte. Ltd.: Singapore, 2016.
35. Nemova, G.; Kashyap, R. Thin-disk athermal laser system. *Opt. Commun.* **2014**, *319*, 100–105. [CrossRef]
36. Yang, Z.; Meng, J.; Albrecht, A.R.; Sheik-Bahae, M. Radiation-balanced Yb:YAG disk laser. *Opt. Express* **2019**, *27*, 1392–1400. [CrossRef]
37. Yang, Z.; Meng, J.; Albrecht, A.R.; Kock, J.; Sheik-Bahae, M. Radiation-balanced thin-disk lasers in Yb:YAG and Yb:YLF. In Proceedings of the SPIE Photonic Heat Engines: Science and Applications, San Francisco, CA, USA, 2–7 February 2019; p. 23.
38. Volpi, A.; Kocka, J.; Albrechta, A.R.; Rostamia, S.; Hehlenb, M.P.; Sheik-Bahae, M. Mode scaling in radiation balanced disk lasers for various gain materials. In Proceedings of the SPIE Photonic Heat Engines: Science and Applications III, Online, 6–12 March 2021; Volume 11702, p. 117020U.
39. Nemova, G.; Kashyap, R. Fiber amplifier with integrated optical cooler. *J. Opt. Soc. Am. B* **2009**, *26*, 2237–2241. [CrossRef]
40. Nemova, G.; Kashyap, R. Raman fiber amplifier with integrated cooler. *IEEE J. Light. Technol.* **2009**, *27*, 5597–5601. [CrossRef]
41. Nemova, G.; Kashyap, R. High-power fiber lasers with integrated rare-earth optical cooler. In Proceedings of the SPIE Laser Refrigeration of Solids III, San Francisco, CA, USA, 23–28 January 2010; Volume 7614, pp. 761406–761416.

2. Mafi, A. Temperature distribution inside a double-cladding optical fiber laser or amplifier. *J. Opt. Soc. Am. B* **2020**, *37*, 1821–1828. [CrossRef]
3. Peysokhan, M.; Mobini, E.; Allahverdi, A.; Abaie, B.; Mafi, A. Characterization of Yb-doped ZBLAN fiber as a platform for radiation-balanced lasers. *Photonics Res.* **2020**, *8*, 202–210. [CrossRef]
4. Peysokhan, M.; Mobini, E.; Mafi, A. Analytical formulation of a high-power Yb-doped double-cladding fiber laser. *OSA Contin.* **2020**, *3*, 1940–1951. [CrossRef]
5. Vigneron, P.B.; Knalla, J.; Boilardb, T.; Bernierb, M.; Digonnet, M.J.F. Observation of anti-Stokes-fluorescence cooling in a ZBLAN fiber with a Yb-doped cladding. In Proceedings of the SPIE OPTO, Online, 5 April 2021; Volume 11702, p. 117020A.
6. Gosnell, T.R. Laser cooling of a solid by 65 K starting from room temperature. *Opt. Lett.* **1999**, *24*, 1041–1043. [CrossRef]
7. Knall, J.M.; Arora, A.; Bernier, M.; Digonnet, M.J.F. Anti-stokes fluorescence cooling in Yb-doped ZBLAN fibers at atmospheric pressure: Experiments and near-future prospects. In Proceedings of the SPIE Photonic Heat Engines: Science and Applications, San Francisco, CA, USA, 2–7 February 2019; Volume 10936, p. 109360F.
8. Knall, J.; Arora, A.; Bernier, M.; Cozic, S.; Digonnet, M.J.F. Demonstration of anti-Stokes cooling in Ybdoped ZBLAN fibers at atmospheric pressure. *Opt. Lett.* **2019**, *44*, 2338–2341. [CrossRef] [PubMed]
9. Arora, A.; Esmaeelpour, M.; Bernier, M.; Digonnet, M.J.F. High-resolution slow-light fiber Bragg grating temperature sensor with phase-sensitive detection. *Opt. Lett.* **2018**, *43*, 3337–3340. [CrossRef] [PubMed]
10. Ytterbium Single-Mode CW Systems. Available online: http://www.ipgphotonics.com/en/products/lasers/high-power-cwfiber-lasers/1-micron/yls-sm-1-10-kw (accessed on 13 August 2021).
11. Aydin, Y.O.; Fortin, V.; Vallée, R.; Bernier, M. Towards power scaling of 2.8 µm fiber lasers. *Opt. Lett.* **2018**, *43*, 4542–4545. [CrossRef]
12. Knall, J.; Vigneron, P.-B.; Engholm, M.; Dragic, P.D.; Yu, N.; Ballato, J.; Bernier, M.; Digonnet, M.J.F. Laser cooling in a silica optical fiber at atmospheric pressure. *Opt. Lett.* **2020**, *45*, 1092–1095. [CrossRef]
13. Mobini, E.; Rostami, S.; Peysokhan, M.; Albrecht, A.; Kuhn, S.; Hein, S.; Hupel, C.; Nold, J.; Haarlammert, N.; Schreiber, T.; et al. Laser cooling in silica glass. *arXiv* **2020**, arXiv:1910.10609v1.
14. Knall, J.; Engholm, M.; Ballato, J.; Dragic, P.D.; Yu, N.; Digonnet, M.J.F. Experimental comparison of silica fibers for laser cooling. *Opt. Lett.* **2002**, *45*, 4020–4023. [CrossRef] [PubMed]
15. Knall, J.M.; Engholm, M.; Boilard, T.; Bernier, M.; Digonnet, M.J.F. A radiation-balanced silica fiber amplifier. *arXiv* **2021**, arXiv:2103.02698.
16. Knall, J.M.; Digonnet, M.J.F. Design of high-power radiation-balanced silica fiber lasers with a doped core and cladding. *J. Light. Technol.* **2021**, *39*, 2497–2504. [CrossRef]
17. Nemova, G.; Kashyap, R. Laser cooling with Tm^{3+}-doped nano-crystals of oxy-fluoride glass ceramic. In Proceedings of the SPIE Photonics Europe, Brussels, Belgium, 1 May 2012; Volume 8424, p. 84242I.
18. Nemova, G.; Kashyap, R. Laser cooling with Tm^{3+}-doped oxy-fluoride glass ceramic. *J. Opt. Soc. Am. B* **2012**, *29*, 3034–3038. [CrossRef]
19. Xia, X.; Pauzauskie, P.J.; Pant, A.; Davis, E.J. Laser refrigeration of optical fibers via optically-active composite cladding materials. In Proceedings of the SPIE Photonic Heat Engines: Science and Applications, San Francisco, CA, USA, 2–7 February 2019; Volume 10936, p. 109360I.
20. Xia, X.; Pant, A.; Davis, E.J.; Pauzauskie, P.J. Design of a radiation-balanced fiber-laser via optically active composite cladding materials. *J. Opt. Soc. Am. B* **2019**, *36*, 3307–3314. [CrossRef]
21. Fernandez-Bravo, A.; Yao, K.; Barnard, E.S.; Borys, N.J.; Levy, E.S.; Tian, B.; Tajon, C.A.; Moretti, L.; Altoe, M.V.; Aloni, S.; et al. Continuous-wave upconverting nanoparticle microlasers. *Nat. Nanotechnol.* **2018**, *13*, 572–577. [CrossRef]
22. Liu, Y.; Teitelboim, A.; Fernandez-Bravo, A.; Yao, K.; Altoe, M.V.P.; Aloni, S.; Zhang, C.; Cohen, B.E.; Schuck, P.J.; Chan, E.M. Controlled Assembly of Upconverting Nanoparticles for Low-Threshold Microlasers and Their Imaging in Scattering Media. *ACS Nano* **2020**, *14*, 1508–1519. [CrossRef]
23. Xiaa, X.; Pantb, A.; Felstedb, R.G.; Gariepyb, R.E.; Davisc, E.J.; Pauzauskie, P.J. Radiation balanced spherical microlaser. In Proceedings of the SPIE Photonic Heat Engines: Science and Applications III, Online, 6–12 March 2021; Volume 11702, p. 117020R.
24. Nakayama, Y.; Harada, Y.; Kita, T. An energy transfer accompanied by phonon absorption in ytterbium-doped yttrium aluminum perovskite for optical refrigeration. *Appl. Phys. Lett.* **2020**, *117*, 041104. [CrossRef]
25. Nakayama, Y.; Harada, Y.; Kita, T. Yb-doped yttrium aluminum perovskite for radiation balanced laser application. In Proceedings of the SPIE Photonic Heat Engines: Science and Applications III, Online, 6–12 March 2021; Volume 11702, p. 117020K.
26. Sheik-Bahae, M.; Yang, Z. Optimum Operation of Radiation-Balanced Lasers. *IEEE J. Quantum Electron.* **2020**, *56*, 1000109. [CrossRef]

Article

Safe and Scalable Polyethylene Glycol-Assisted Hydrothermal Synthesis and Laser Cooling of 10%Yb^{3+}:LiLuF$_4$ Crystals

Elena A. Dobretsova [1,2], Anupum Pant [1,3], Xiaojing Xia [4], Rachel E. Gariepy [1] and Peter J. Pauzauskie [1,5,*]

1. Department of Materials Science & Engineering, University of Washington, Seattle, WA 98195, USA; elenadobretsova89@gmail.com (E.A.D.); anupum.pant@gmail.com (A.P.); rachelg2@uw.edu (R.E.G.)
2. Prokhorov General Physics Institute of the Russian Academy of Sciences, 119991 Moscow, Russia
3. Intel Corporation, Hillsboro, OR 97124, USA
4. Molecular Engineering and Science Institute, University of Washington, Seattle, WA 98195, USA; xiaxj@uw.edu
5. Physical Sciences Division, Physical and Computational Sciences Directorate, Pacific Northwest National Laboratory, Richland, WA 99352, USA
* Correspondence: peterpz@uw.edu; Tel.: +1-(206)-543-2303

Featured Application: A safe and scalable method is reported for the synthesis of rare earth doped lithium fluorides that allows for much larger bulk syntheses of these materials that would be challenging when using more hazardous reagents.

Abstract: Rare earth doped lithium fluorides are a class of materials with a wide variety of optical applications, but the hazardous reagents used in their synthesis often restrict the amount of product that can be created at one time. In this work, 10%Yb^{3+}:LiLuF$_4$ (Yb:LLF) crystals have been synthesized through a safe and scalable polyethylene glycol (PEG)-assisted hydrothermal method. A combination of X-ray diffraction (XRD) analysis, scanning electron microscopy (SEM), and photoluminescence (PL) measurements were used to characterize the obtained materials. The influence of reaction temperature, time, fluoride source, and precursor amount on the shape and size of the Yb:LLF crystals are also discussed. Calibrated PL spectra of Yb^{3+} ions show laser cooling to more than 15 K below room temperature in air and 5 K in deionized water under 1020 nm diode laser excitation measured at a laser power of 50 mW.

Keywords: laser refrigeration; hydrothermal synthesis; crystal growth; ratiometric thermometry

Citation: Dobretsova, E.A.; Pant, A.; Xia, X.; Gariepy, R.E.; Pauzauskie, P.J. Safe and Scalable Polyethylene Glycol-Assisted Hydrothermal Synthesis and Laser Cooling of 10%Yb^{3+}:LiLuF$_4$ Crystals. *Appl. Sci.* **2022**, *12*, 774. https://doi.org/10.3390/app12020774

Academic Editor: Galina Nemova

Received: 27 November 2021
Accepted: 8 January 2022
Published: 13 January 2022

Publisher's Note: MDPI stays neutral with regard to jurisdictional claims in published maps and institutional affiliations.

Copyright: © 2022 by the authors. Licensee MDPI, Basel, Switzerland. This article is an open access article distributed under the terms and conditions of the Creative Commons Attribution (CC BY) license (https://creativecommons.org/licenses/by/4.0/).

1. Introduction

Rare earth lithium fluorides (RELiF$_4$) with a scheelite structure are widely used in various fields such as theranostics [1], long-term in vivo bioimaging [2,3], photothermal therapy [4–6], ratiometric temperature sensing [7], transparent volumetric displays [8,9], multi-level anti-counterfeiting applications [10], photocatalysis [11], photovoltaics [12], scintillating materials [13], and refrigeration through laser radiation [14–20]. These materials also show promise for solid-state laser applications [21].

Recently, it has been demonstrated that low-cost, low-temperature hydrothermal processing can be used to grow YLiF$_4$ [17], NaYF$_4$ [22], KLuF$_4$ [23], and LiLuF$_4$ [24] crystals that are capable of solid-state laser refrigeration. However, the use of ammonium bifluoride inhibits the production of large amounts of these materials due to the danger of hydrofluoric acid formation in solution, which can then form gaseous hydrogen fluoride during the autoclave portion of the synthesis. Using polyethylene glycol (PEG) in place of NH$_4$HF$_2$ helps improve the solubility of lithium ions while also reducing potential hazards posed by the use of ammonium bifluoride and, as a result, makes this method safer and more scalable.

Due to the complexity of hydrothermal systems, various internal and external factors can fundamentally affect the purity, crystal structure, morphology, and physical properties of the obtained materials. For example, it has been shown that LiOH concentration is the key factor responsible for the shape evolution and phase control of RELiF$_4$ nanocrystals at selected temperatures [25]. It has also been shown that the use of EDTA as a chelating agent in the reaction is essential to obtain highly crystalline and smooth Er^{3+}:LiYbF$_4$ microparticles [26]. Most importantly, these hydrothermal materials show more efficient luminescence with further heat treatment. Higher reaction temperatures and prolonged reaction times have been shown to facilitate the formation of more stable LiYbF$_4$ microcrystals [27]. The substitution of Li$^+$ in Na$_{(1-x)}$Li$_x$ReF$_4$ not only causes a phase transition but also induces variation in the morphology, size, and luminescent properties of the final microcrystals [28]. Taking these observations into consideration, parameters other than the fluoride source, such as temperature, precursor amount, and reaction length, must be carefully controlled and examined to determine their effect on the final crystal.

In this work, we report a method for PEG-assisted hydrothermal synthesis of Yb^{3+}-doped lithium lutetium fluoride (Yb:LLF) microcrystals and discuss the influence of various factors on the growth of the Yb:LLF microcrystals and their ability to undergo laser refrigeration.

2. Materials and Methods

Synthesis of 10%Yb^{3+}:LiLuF$_4$. The reagents used in this synthesis are identical to those used in a similar synthesis in previous work [24].

The following synthesis (Figure 1) is a slight modification of previous work [17]. In contrast to the referenced procedure, yttrium nitrate (Lu(NO$_3$)) and ytterbium nitrate (Yb(NO$_3$)) of 99.999% purity were used as purchased from Sigma-Aldrich. The nitrate powders were dissolved in Millipore deionized (DI) water to achieve a stock concentration of the respective nitrates. Additionally, nitric acid (HNO$_3$) and ammonium bifluoride (NH$_4$HF$_2$) were not used in this synthesis. Lithium fluoride (LiF) and polyethylene glycol (PEG, M_n = 4000) were used directly without any purification. For this synthesis, 28.8 mL of 0.5 M Lu(NO$_3$)$_3$ and 3.2 mL of 0.5 M Yb(NO$_3$)$_3$ were mixed with 16 mmol of EDTA and 30 mmol of LiOH in 20 mL of Millipore DI water at 50 °C while stirring for 30 min to form solution A. Subsequently, 64 mmol of LiF were dissolved in 30 mL of 10 wt.% PEG Millipore DI water solution at room temperature while stirring for 1 h to form solution B. Solutions A and B were mixed together while stirring for 30 min to form a homogeneous white suspension, which was transferred to a 2-L Teflon-lined autoclave and heated to 180 °C for 24 h. After the autoclave cooled to room temperature, the Yb:LLF particles were recovered by centrifuging and washing with ethanol and Millipore DI water three times. The final white powder was obtained by calcining at 300 °C for 2 h in air, which was determined to be the ideal temperature for calcination via XRD and SEM (Figures S1 and S2). The theoretical yield was 4.120 g of Yb:LLF. The actual yield was 2.0 g, for a yield percentage of 48.5%

Multiple variations of this base synthesis were performed to examine the effects of different variables on the crystals. In some experiments, the reagent amounts were reduced by a factor of 4. Other syntheses were performed at temperatures other than 180 °C, including 100, 120, 130, 200, and 220 °C for 24 h. The effect of time on the synthesis was also examined, with data from some syntheses collected at 3 h, 5 h, and 14 h, as well as the standard 24 h time point.

Characterization. Scanning electron microscopy (SEM) images were taken on an FEI Sirion XL30 SEM at an accelerating voltage of 15 keV. Powder X-ray diffraction (XRD) patterns were obtained on the Bruker F8 Focus Powder XRD with Cu K-α (40 kV, 40 mA) irradiation (λ = 0.154 nm). The 2θ angle of the XRD data was 16° to 93°, and the scanning rate was 0.36° s^{-1}. PL spectra were registered following a method outlined in previous work [24].

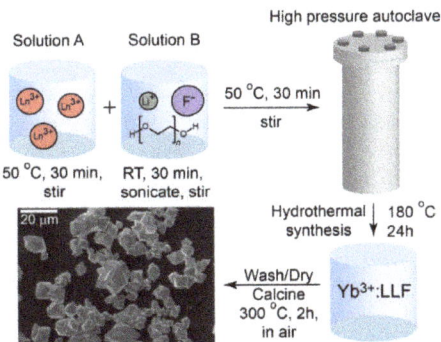

Figure 1. Schematic of the base PEG-assisted hydrothermal synthesis of Yb:LLF microcrystals.

When collecting photoluminescence spectra, Yb:LLF crystals were attached to optical fibers for the sake of thermal isolation. The crystals were then optically excited in air using a 1020 nm diode laser with irradiances ranging from 0.08 to 1 MW/cm^2. Temperatures were calibrated for individual Yb:LLF grains using an optical cryostat. Temperatures were scanned from 300 to 400 K with a low laser irradiance of 0.04 MW/cm^2 to minimize any photothermal effects caused by optical excitation. Cold Brownian motion data were collected using a home-built optical trapping setup and following a procedure from previous work [17].

3. Results

Scanning electron microscopy (SEM) of two different Yb:LLF crystals are shown in Figure 2a. In the first case (Figure 2a), the Yb:LLF crystals have been synthesized through an NH_4HF_2-assisted hydrothermal method [17,24]. They have a tetragonal bipyramidal morphology with a dominating (101) surface. The Yb:LLF crystals synthesized through the PEG-assisted hydrothermal method (Figure 2b) have two dominating surfaces: (101) and (112), respectively, which was predicted in Littleford's works [29,30] for a yttrium lithium fluoride (YLF) crystal. Figure S3 also shows the room-temperature FTIR spectra of the Yb:LLF crystals obtained at different conditions. The weak peaks in the FTIR spectra can be attributed to atmospheric water and carbon dioxide adsorbed on the optical elements of the spectrometer and on the samples, and the absence of strong bands in the range of 1000–4000 cm^{-1} implies that there is no residual PEG and minimal oxyfluorides on the surface of the crystals regardless of synthesis method.

X-ray diffraction analysis confirms that crystals from both syntheses adopt a tetragonal scheelite structure (ICDD number 04-002-3255) with space group $I4_1/a$ (Figure 2c). Comparison of the two X-ray diffraction spectra of Yb:LLF (Figure 2c) corresponding to NH_4HF_2- (blue) and PEG-assisted (red) syntheses gives different ratios of $I(101){:}I(112)$, which correlates with the morphology of the Yb:LLF crystals. Stereographic projections of crystal facets related to the most intensive XRD peaks are shown in Figure 2d (inset) as red circles.

Crystals grown using the base PEG-assisted synthesis described previously were subjected to photoluminescence (PL) measurements to examine the cooling abilities of the crystals grown via this new method. Crystals grown via the base synthesis method were used due to the method's ability to consistently produce pure single crystals with only one phase. This avoids issues caused by parasitic energy transfer or luminescence quenching due to impurities, maximizing the laser cooling power of the crystals. The PL spectra obtained at different 1020 nm laser powers are shown in Figure 3a. Changes in the ratio of the integrated emission bands R_1 and R_2 (and their respective intensities in a.u., I_1, and I_2), which stem from transitions between energy states E_6-E_1 and E_5-$E_{2,3}$, respectively, are directly correlated to a change in the crystal temperature through a Boltzmann distribution

(Figure 3b). Ratiometric spectral measurements were used to calibrate temperature in which $\ln(I_1/I_2)$ varies linearly with $1/T$ (calibration shown in Figure S4). The decrease in the logarithmic ratio of I_1 to I_2 with increasing irradiance reflects a decrease in the internal lattice temperature of approximately 15 K below room temperature (Figure 3b) Analogous laser cooling trends (approximately 5 K below room temperature) were observed for individual Yb:LLF grains optically trapped in water (Figure 3c). These values are comparable to cooling temperatures Yb:LLF crystals obtained via the NH_4HF_2-assisted synthesis. [24] Additionally, these crystals exhibit much greater cooling capability than 5%-Yb doped LLF crystals grown via the Czochralski process but do not cool to the cryogenic temperatures reached by Czochralski-grown Yb:YLF crystals [15,31].

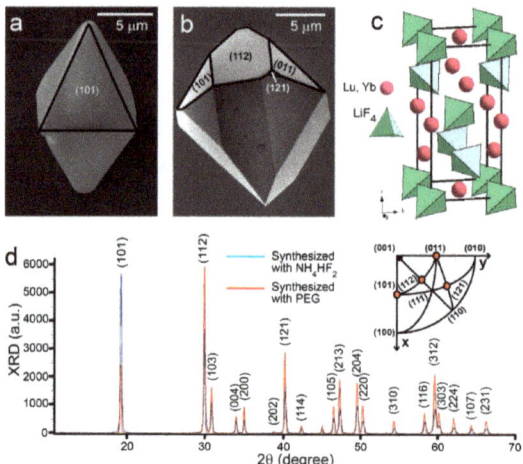

Figure 2. Characterization of Yb:LLF crystals. Scanning electron microscope images of faceted Yb:LLF particles synthesized with NH_4HF_2- (**a**) and PEG-assisted (**b**) hydrothermal syntheses. Scale bar = 5 µm. Types of facets are indicated in parentheses. (**c**) Schematic of a Scheelite crystal structure of Yb:LLF with $I4_1/a$ space group symmetry. (**d**) Powder XRD pattern of Yb:LLF crystals following NH_4HF_2- (blue) and PEG-assisted (red) hydrothermal synthesis, indicating a Scheelite crystal structure. Inset: stereographic projections of crystal facets related to the most intensive XRD peaks.

Reducing the concentration of reagents by a factor of four leads to the synthesis of significantly smaller crystals. The low concentration synthesis produced crystals around 5 µm in size, whereas the standard synthesis could produce crystals as large as 20 µm. Although their size is greatly changed, the morphology of the crystals remains the same regardless of the reagent concentration. The (112) plane remains clearly visible on both sets of crystals (Figure S5).

XRD data from a range of experimental temperatures spanning from 100 °C to 200 °C are shown in Figure 4. At lower temperatures, a variety of side products can be seen in the XRD data, including LuF_3 and $LiLuO_2$. Unreacted or undissolved LiF can also be seen in many of the XRD patterns. A stable, single phase of Yb:LLF is not reached after 24 h unless the standard reaction temperature of 180 °C or above is used. Additionally, the size of the formed crystals also increases with reaction temperature, which can be seen in SEM images (Figure S6). Reaction time also plays a factor in the generation of a single, stable Yb:LLF phase. At lower time points, the XRD data shows mostly unreacted LiF and little to no evidence of the Yb:LLF crystals. After 14 h, a significant Yb:LLF phase can be seen, and only traces of LiF remain (Figure S7). SEM also shows that increasing the length of the synthesis causes the crystal facets and morphology to be more well-defined and fully formed (Figure S8).

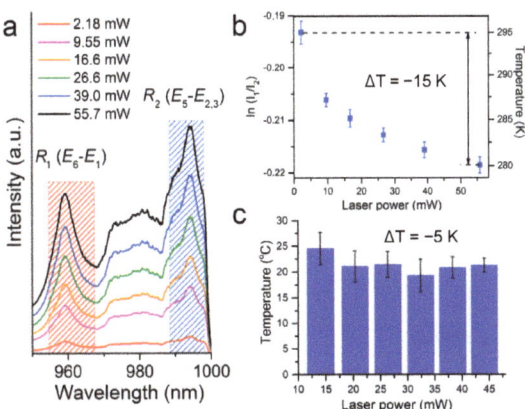

Figure 3. Laser cooling of Yb:LLF crystals. (**a**) PL spectra of the Yb:LLF crystal on a SiO$_2$ optical fiber in air under 1020 nm diode laser excitation measured at different irradiances. (**b**) Cryostat calibration of PL spectra of the Yb:LLF crystal on a SiO$_2$ optical fiber in air under 1020 nm diode laser excitation measured at different irradiances. (**c**) Laser refrigeration of the Yb:LLF crystal in deionized water measured via cold Brownian motion analysis at different irradiances.

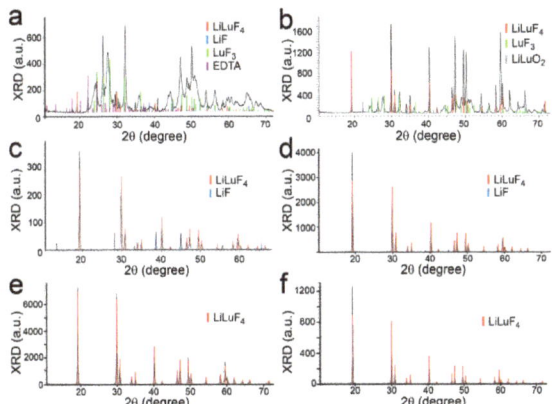

Figure 4. Powder XRD pattern of crystals following PEG-assisted hydrothermal synthesis at: (**a**) 100 °C, (**b**) 120 °C, (**c**) 130 °C, (**d**) 150 °C, (**e**) 180 °C, and (**f**) 200 °C, for 24 h.

4. Discussion

The fluoride source and inclusion of PEG clearly affect the morphology of the Yb:LLF crystals. The (112) planes seen in all crystals synthesized via the PEG-assisted method indicate that the PEG lowers the surface energy of that plane, changing the Wulff construction of the crystal and allowing it to form during the hydrothermal synthesis. In spite of this additional plane, the stoichiometric 1:1:4 product is formed, as confirmed by XRD. This is of particular interest as other RELiF$_4$ materials, such as NaYF$_4$, do not form a stoichiometric phase. [32] Additionally, this extra plane does not impact the crystals' cooling abilities, which are comparable to those shown by crystals formed using the ammonium bifluoride synthesis. It can then be concluded that this synthesis method is not only effective, but a safe and scalable alternative to the ammonium bifluoride synthesis when attempting to synthesize large amounts of Yb:LLF crystals. This synthesis generates high amounts of product while avoiding the hazards of hydrofluoric acid formation and hydrogen fluoride gas generation.

Compared to the fluoride source, the temperature and length of the reaction do not significantly impact crystal morphology but, instead, are key factors in forming a pure and highly crystalline Yb:LLF phase, as well as impacting the size of the crystals formed. The number of precursors remaining in solution at shorter time points, specifically undissolved or unreacted LiF, could be eliminated by allowing the reaction to proceed for longer times, further improving the yield of the reaction. The size of the crystals can also be controlled by the concentration of precursors in an aqueous solution. By combining the size control demonstrated by changing the reaction temperature and the size control demonstrated by the precursor concentrations, it could be possible to finely control the size of the crystals.

5. Conclusions

Yb:LLF crystals with a scheelite structure (space group $I4_1/a$) have been synthesized through a safe and scalable PEG-assisted hydrothermal approach. We show that size and morphology can be finely controlled by changing reaction conditions such as temperature, time, fluoride source, and precursor amount. The results show that higher temperature and prolonged reaction time facilitate the formation of more stable $LiLuF_4$ crystals. The substitution of PEG for NH_4HF_2 changes the morphology of the product, as shown by the appearance of crystal facets (101) and (112) in the PEG-assisted crystals. The average size of the crystals can be controlled by the concentration of precursors in an aqueous solution. We demonstrate solid-state laser refrigeration of the Yb:LLF crystals using a focused near-infrared laser excitation source ($\lambda = 1020$ nm). A calibrated ratiometric Boltzmann analysis of the Yb^{3+} luminescence reveals laser cooling in air by more than 15 K below room temperature and in water by more than 5 K below room temperature.

Supplementary Materials: The following supporting information can be downloaded at: https://www.mdpi.com/article/10.3390/app12020774/s1, Figure S1: Scanning electron microscope images of crystals following PEG-assisted hydrothermal synthesis at: (a) 100 °C (scale bar is 1 µm), (b) 120 °C (scale bar is 1 µm), (c) 130 °C (scale bar is 1 µm), (d) 180 °C (scale bar is 2 µm), (e) 200 °C (scale bar is 2 µm) and (f) 220 °C (scale bar is 5 µm), for 24 h, Figure S2: Powder XRD pattern of crystals following PEG-assisted hydrothermal synthesis at 130 °C for: (a) 3 h, (b) 5 h, (c) 14 h, (d) 24 h, Figure S3: Scanning electron microscope images of crystals following PEG-assisted hydrothermal synthesis at 130 °C for: (a) 3 h (scale bar is 1 µm), (b) 5 h (500 nm), (c) 14 h (1 µm), (d) 24 h (1 µm), Figure S4: Temperature-calibrated PL spectra of Yb^{3+}:LLF, Figure S5: ATR-FTIR spectra of Yb^{3+}:LLF synthesized under following conditions: (a) at 130 °C for 14 h; (b) at 150 °C for 5 h; (c) at 200 °C for 24 h; (d) at 200 °C for 72 h; (e) at 220 °C for 5 h; (f) at 220 °C for 48 h, Figure S6: Powder XRD pattern of crystals following PEG-assisted hydrothermal synthesis at 220 °C for 2 h (a) without calcination and calcination at: (b) 300 °C, (c) 500 °C, (d) 600 °C, Figure S7: Scanning electron microscope images of crystals following PEG-assisted hydrothermal synthesis at 220 °C for 2 h (a) without calcination and calcination at: (b) 300 °C, (c) 500 °C h, (d) 600 °C. Scale bar is 1 µm, Figure S8: Scanning electron microscope images of LLF crystals following PEG-assisted hydrothermal synthesis at 200 °C for 24 h. (a) RE nitrate precursor amount is 4 mmol. Scale bar is 5 µm. (b) RE nitrate precursor amount is 16 mmol. Scale bar is 20 µm.

Author Contributions: Conceptualization, E.A.D. and P.J.P.; methodology, E.A.D. and P.J.P.; software, E.A.D., A.P. and X.X.; validation, R.E.G.; formal analysis, E.A.D., A.P. and X.X.; investigation, E.A.D., A.P., X.X. and R.E.G.; resources, P.J.P.; data curation, E.A.D., X.X., A.P. and R.E.G.; writing—original draft preparation, E.A.D.; writing—review and editing, E.A.D., A.P., X.X., R.E.G. and P.J.P.; visualization, E.A.D., A.P. and X.X.; supervision, E.A.D. and P.J.P.; project administration, E.A.D. and P.J.P.; funding acquisition, P.J.P. All authors have read and agreed to the published version of the manuscript.

Funding: E.A.D., R.E.G. and P.J.P. acknowledge support from the National Science Foundation through the UW Molecular Engineering Materials Center, a Materials Research Science and Engineering Center (DMR-1719797). A.P., X.X. and P.J.P. acknowledge financial support from the MURI:MARBLe project under the auspices of the Air Force Office of Scientific Research (Award No. FA9550-16-1-0362). Part of this work was conducted at the Molecular Analysis Facility, a National Nanotech-ology Coordinated Infrastructure site at the University of Washington, which is supported in part by the National Science Foundation (grant ECC-1542101).

Institutional Review Board Statement: Not applicable.

Informed Consent Statement: Not applicable.

Data Availability Statement: The data presented in this study are available on request from the corresponding author.

Acknowledgments: We acknowledge Mikhail Kosobokov (N.D. Zelinsky Institute of Organic Chemistry of the Russian Academy of Sciences) for his useful recommendations for hydrothermal synthesis of the Yb:LLF crystals.

Conflicts of Interest: The authors declare no conflict of interest.

References

1. Skripka, A.; Karabanovas, V.; Jarockyte, G.; Marin, R.; Tam, V.; Cerruti, M.; Rotomskis, R.; Vetrone, F. Decoupling theranostics with rare earth doped nanoparticles. *Adv. Funct. Mater.* **2019**, *29*, 1807105. [CrossRef]
2. Huang, P.; Zheng, W.; Zhou, S.; Tu, D.; Chen, Z.; Zhu, H.; Li, R.; Ma, E.; Huang, M.; Chen, X. Lanthanide-doped LiLuF$_4$ upconversion nanoprobes for the detection of disease biomarkers. *Angew. Chem. Int. Ed.* **2014**, *53*, 1252–1257. [CrossRef] [PubMed]
3. Qin, Q.-S.; Zhang, P.-Z.; Sun, L.-D.; Shi, S.; Chen, N.-X.; Dong, H.; Zheng, X.-Y.; Li, L.-M.; Yan, C.-H. Ultralow-power near-infrared excited neodymium-doped nanoparticles for long-term in vivo bioimaging. *Nanoscale* **2017**, *9*, 4660–4664. [CrossRef] [PubMed]
4. Tsuboi, T.; Shimamura, K. Temperature sensitive near-infrared luminescence of Er^{3+} ions in LiYF$_4$. *Phys. Status Solidi C* **2011**, *8*, 2833–2836. [CrossRef]
5. Skripka, A.; Morinvil, A.; Matulionyte, M.; Cheng, T.; Vetrone, F. Advancing neodymium single-band nanothermometry. *Nanoscale* **2019**, *11*, 11322–11330. [CrossRef]
6. Meijer, M.S.; Rojas-Gutierrez, P.A.; Busko, D.; Howard, I.A.; Frenzel, F.; Würth, C.; Resch-Genger, U.; Richards, B.S.; Turshatov, A.; Capobianco, J.A.; et al. Absolute upconversion quantum yields of blue-emitting LiYF$_4$:Yb^{3+}, Tm^{3+} upconverting nanoparticles. *Phys. Chem. Chem. Phys.* **2018**, *20*, 22556–22562. [CrossRef] [PubMed]
7. Huang, P.; Zheng, W.; Tu, D.; Shang, X.; Zhang, M.; Li, R.; Xu, J.; Liu, Y.; Chen, X. Unraveling the electronic structures of neodymium in LiLuF$_4$ nanocrystals for ratiometric temperature sensing. *Adv. Sci.* **2019**, *6*, 1802282. [CrossRef] [PubMed]
8. Shin, J.; Kyhm, J.-H.; Hong, A.-R.; Song, J.D.; Lee, K.; Ko, H.; Jang, H.S. Multicolor tunable upconversion luminescence from sensitized seed-mediated grown LiGdF$_4$:Yb, Tm-based core/triple-shell nanophosphors for transparent displays. *Chem. Mater.* **2018**, *30*, 8457–8464. [CrossRef]
9. Kim, S.Y.; Won, Y.-H.; Jang, H.S. A strategy to enhance Eu^{3+} emission from LiYF$_4$:Eu nanophosphors and green-to-orange multicolor tunable, transparent nanophosphor-polymer composites. *Sci. Rep.* **2015**, *5*, 7866. [CrossRef]
10. Gao, W.; Wang, R.; Han, Q.; Dong, J.; Yan, L.; Zheng, H. Tuning red upconversion emission in single LiYF$_4$:Yb^{3+}/Ho^{3+} microparticle. *J. Phys. Chem. C* **2015**, *119*, 2349–2355. [CrossRef]
11. Cheng, T.; Marin, R.; Skripka, A.; Vetrone, F. Small and bright lithium-based upconverting nanoparticles. *J. Am. Chem. Soc.* **2018**, *140*, 12890–12899. [CrossRef]
12. Chen, X.; Xu, W.; Song, H.; Chen, C.; Xia, H.; Zhu, Y.; Zhou, D.; Cui, S.; Dai, Q.; Zhang, J. Highly efficient LiYF$_4$:Yb^{3+}, Er^{3+} upconversion single crystal under solar cell spectrum excitation and photovoltaic application. *ACS Appl. Mater. Interfaces* **2016**, *8*, 9071–9079. [CrossRef]
13. Mahalingam, V.; Naccache, R.; Vetrone, F.; Capobianco, J.A. Sensitized Ce^{3+} and Gd^{3+} ultraviolet emissions by Tm^{3+} in colloidal LiYF$_4$ nanocrystals. *Chem.–A Eur. J.* **2009**, *15*, 9660–9663. [CrossRef] [PubMed]
14. Seletskiy, D.V.; Melgaard, S.D.; Bigotta, S.; Di Lieto, A.; Tonelli, M.; Sheik-Bahae, M. Laser cooling of solids to cryogenic temperatures. *Nat. Photonics* **2010**, *4*, 161. [CrossRef]
15. Melgaard, S.D.; Seletskiy, D.V.; Di Lieto, A.; Tonelli, M.; Sheik-Bahae, M. Optical refrigeration to 119 K, below national institute of standards and technology cryogenic temperature. *Opt. Lett.* **2013**, *38*, 1588. [CrossRef] [PubMed]
16. Rahman, A.A.; Barker, P. Laser refrigeration, alignment and rotation of levitated Yb^{3+}:YLF nanocrystals. *Nat. Photonics* **2017**, *11*, 634. [CrossRef]
17. Roder, P.B.; Smith, B.E.; Zhou, X.; Crane, M.J.; Pauzauskie, P.J. Laser refrigeration of hydrothermal nanocrystals in physiological media. *Proc. Natl. Acad. Sci. USA* **2015**, *112*, 15024–15029. [CrossRef]

18. Xia, X.; Pant, A.; Davis, E.J.; Pauzauskie, P.J. Design of a radiation-balanced fiber laser via optically active composite cladding materials. *J. Opt. Soc. Am. B* **2019**, *36*, 3307–3314. [CrossRef]
19. Pant, A.; Xia, X.; Davis, E.J.; Pauzauskie, P.J. Solid-state laser refrigeration of a composite semiconductor Yb:YLiF$_4$ optomechanical resonator. *Nat. Commun.* **2020**, *11*, 3235. [CrossRef] [PubMed]
20. Xia, X.; Pant, A.; Ganas, A.S.; Jelezko, F.; Pauzauskie, P.J. Quantum point defects for solid-state laser refrigeration. *Adv. Mater.* **2021**, *33*, 1905406. [CrossRef]
21. Yasyukevich, A.S.; Mandrik, A.V.; Kuleshov, N.V.; Gordeev, E.Y.; Korableva, S.L.; Naumov, A.K.; Semashko, V.V.; Popov, P.A. Spectral kinetic properties of Yb^{3+}:Na$_4$Y$_6$F$_{22}$ and Yb^{3+}:LiLuF$_4$ crystals. *J. Appl. Spectrosc.* **2007**, *74*, 844–850. [CrossRef]
22. Zhou, X.; Smith, B.E.; Roder, P.B.; Pauzauskie, P.J. Laser refrigeration of ytterbium-doped sodium–yttrium–fluoride nanowires. *Adv. Mater.* **2016**, *28*, 8658–8662. [CrossRef]
23. Xia, X.; Pant, A.; Zhou, X.; Dobretsova, E.A.; Bard, A.B.; Lim, M.B.; Roh, J.Y.D.; Gamelin, D.R.; Pauzauskie, P.J. Hydrothermal synthesis and solid-state laser refrigeration of ytterbium-doped potassium-lutetium-fluoride (KLF) microcrystals. *Chem. Mater.* **2021**, *33*, 4417–4424. [CrossRef]
24. Dobretsova, E.A.; Xia, X.; Pant, A.; Lim, M.B.; De Siena, M.C.; Boldyrev, K.N.; Molchanova, A.D.; Novikova, N.N.; Klimin, S.A.; Popova, M.N. Hydrothermal synthesis of Yb^{3+}: LuLiF$_4$ microcrystals and laser refrigeration of Yb^{3+}: LuLiF$_4$/silicon-nitride composite nanostructures. *Laser Photonics Rev.* **2021**, *15*, 2100019. [CrossRef]
25. Zhang, Q.; Yan, B. Hydrothermal synthesis and characterization of LiREF$_4$ (RE = Y, Tb−Lu) nanocrystals and their core−shell nanostructures. *Inorg. Chem.* **2010**, *49*, 6834–6839. [CrossRef] [PubMed]
26. Lu, C.; Huang, W.; Ni, Y.; Xu, Z. Hydrothermal synthesis and luminescence properties of octahedral LiYbF$_4$:Er^{3+} microcrystals. *Mater. Res. Bull.* **2011**, *46*, 216–221. [CrossRef]
27. Huang, W.; Lu, C.; Jiang, C.; Jin, J.; Ding, M.; Ni, Y.; Xu, Z. Rare earth doped LiYbF$_4$ phosphors with controlled morphologies: Hydrothermal synthesis and luminescent properties. *Mater. Res. Bull.* **2012**, *47*, 1310–1315. [CrossRef]
28. Luo, R.; Li, T.; Chen, Y.; Ning, Z.; Zhao, Y.; Liu, M.; Lai, X.; Zhong, C.; Wang, C.; Bi, J.; et al. Na$_{(1-x)}$Li$_x$(Gd$_{0.39}$Y$_{0.39}$Yb$_{0.2}$Er$_{0.02}$)f$_4$ ($0 \leq x \leq 1$) solid solution microcrystals: Li/Na ratio-induced transition of crystalline phase and morphology and their enhanced upconversion emission. *Cryst. Growth Des.* **2018**, *18*, 6581–6590. [CrossRef]
29. Littleford, T.E.; Jackson, R.A.; Read, M.S.D. An atomistic simulation study of the effect of dopants on the morphology of YLiF$_4$. *Phys. Status Solidi C* **2013**, *10*, 156–159. [CrossRef]
30. Littleford, T.E.; Jackson, R.A.; Read, M.S. An atomistic surface simulation study predicting morphologies and segregation in yttrium lithium fluoride. *Surf. Sci.* **2012**, *606*, 1550–1555. [CrossRef]
31. Azzurra, V.; Giovanni, C.; Alberto Di, L.; Arlete, C.; Hans, P.J.; Mauro, T. Investigation of yb-doped LiLuF$_4$ single crystals for optical cooling. *Opt. Eng.* **2016**, *56*, 1–5.
32. Fedorov, P.P.; Aleksandrov, V.B.; Bondareva, O.S.; Buchinskaya, I.I.; Val'Kovskii, M.D.; Sobolev, B.P. Concentration dependences of the unit-cell parameters of nonstoichiometric fluorite-type Na$_{0.5-x}$R$_{0.5+x}$F$_{2+2x}$ phases (R = rare-earth elements). *Crystallogr. Rep.* **2001**, *46*, 239–245. [CrossRef]

Article

Accurate Characterization of the Properties of the Rare-Earth-Doped Crystal for Laser Cooling

Xuelu Duan, Biao Zhong *, Yongqing Lei, Chaoyu Wang, Jiajin Xu, Ziheng Zhang, Jingxin Ding and Jianping Yin *

State Key Laboratory of Precision Spectroscopy, East China Normal University, Shanghai 200062, China; 51190920002@stu.ecnu.edu.cn (X.D.); 52170920007@stu.ecnu.edu.cn (Y.L.); chaoyuwang@foxmail.com (C.W.); 51210920048@stu.ecnu.edu.cn (J.X.); zzh20210314@163.com (Z.Z.); jxding@phy.ecnu.edu.cn (J.D.)
* Correspondence: bzhong@lps.ecnu.edu.cn (B.Z.); jpyin@phy.ecnu.edu.cn (J.Y.)

Abstract: We present a method for calibrating a commercial thermal camera adopted to accurately measure the temperature change of the sample in a laser-induced temperature modulation spectrum (LITMoS) test, which is adopted for measuring two crucial parameters of the external quantum efficiency η_{ext} and the background absorption coefficient α_b for assessing the laser cooling grade of the rare-earth-doped materials. After calibration, the temperature resolution of the calibrated thermal camera is better than 0.1 K. For the cooling grade Czochralski-grown 5% Yb^{3+}:LuLiF$_4$ crystal, the corresponding values of η_{ext} and α_b are LITMoS = measured to be $\eta_{ext} = 99.4\ (\pm 0.1)\%$ and $\alpha_b = 1.5\ (\pm 0.1) \times 10^{-4}\ \text{cm}^{-1}$, respectively.

Keywords: laser cooling; optical cooling; fluoride crystal

1. Introduction

Optical cooling of solids is based on the anti-Stokes fluorescence principle, in which the average wavelength of fluorescence (λ_f) emitted by a transparent solid is shorter than the wavelength of the coherent light (λ) for excitation [1,2]. The extra energy of the fluorescence over the excitation light comes from the kinetic energy of the lattice vibrations in the substrate [3]. The kinetic energy of the lattice vibrations is continuously pumped away, causing a temperature drop of the substrate until the cooling effect is balanced by the heating effect [4–7]. Optical cooling of solids is effective for developing both the cryogenic optical refrigerator of free vibration with high reliability and radiation-balanced lasers (RBLs) of no gain medium heating from quantum defects and non-radiative attenuation [8–14].

R. Epstein and co-workers first demonstrated the anti-Stokes fluorescence cooling concept on the 1 wt.% Yb^{3+}-doped ZBLANP fluoride glass in 1995 [1]. Since then, researchers have focused on exploring new promising potential materials for cryogenic optical cooling. So far, net cooling by laser has been demonstrated not only in a variety of rare-earth-doped (Yb^{3+}-, Tm^{3+}-, Er^{3+}- and Ho^{3+}-) bulk and nano crystals [2,15–31], but also in glassy materials [32–34] and semiconductors of nano structure [35–37]. Among all the crystals tested, fluoride crystals have exhibited the best cooling performances [38–40]. The Yb^{3+}/Tm^{3+} co-doped LiYF$_4$ crystal has been cooled to a record temperature of 87 K [41] and the Yb^{3+} doped LuLiF$_4$ crystal has the potential to be cooled to 89 K [29]. Recently, the Yb^{3+} doped fibers (such as ZBLAN and silica fibers) have been attracting researchers as the platform for RBLs. Especially, the fibers can be further improved in purity and doped with modifiers to increase the Yb ion solubility [42,43]. Demonstration of RBLs and radiation-balanced amplifiers based on the fiber platform has also been reported [14,44,45].

M. Sheik-Bahae and R. Epstein developed a four-level model in theory to describe the laser-cooling processes of rare-earth-doped hosts with four parameters: the external quantum efficiency η_{ext}, the resonant absorption coefficient $\alpha_r(\lambda, T)$, the background absorption coefficient α_b and the mean fluorescence wavelengths $\lambda_f(T)$ being derived for characterizing their cooling performances [7]. Accurate characterization of the laser cooling properties in both theory and experiment is very important for determining high-cooling-grade materials [46–48]. The external quantum efficiency η_{ext} and the background absorption coefficient α_b are two crucial parameters for assessing the laser cooling grade of a material. The laser-induced temperature modulation spectrum (LITMoS) method has been developed to accurately measure these two parameters [48]. The laser-cooling limits of both rare-earth doped fluoride glass of ZBLAN(P) and fluoride crystal of LiYF$_4$ were accurately predicted from their corresponding "cooling windows" obtained with the help of the LITMoS method [41,42,48–50]. For instance, the minimum achievable temperature (MAT) of the Yb^{3+}-doped LiYF$_4$ crystal was predicted to be as low as 60 K, which is lower than the temperature of liquid nitrogen [41,51,52]. However, the MAT of the Yb^{3+}-doped ZBLAN glass was estimated to be only about 200 K [33]. Recently, a Yb^{3+}/Tm^{3+} co-doped LiYF$_4$ crystal picked up by LITMoS test was used to cool a Fourier Transform Infrared detector (HgCdTe) down to 135 K [53,54].

Here we adopt the LITMoS method at room temperature to accurately characterize a sample material in its external quantum efficiency η_{ext} and background absorption coefficient α_b, two crucial laser-cooling parameters for assessing its corresponding cooling grade. The accuracy of the characterization depends on the precise measurement in situ of the laser-induced temperature change of the sample. A well-calibrated thermal camera is adopted to contactlessly measure the temperature of the sample in the LITMoS test. The calibration of the thermal camera is described in detail with a temperature resolution better than 0.1 K. The cooling window of a Czochralski-grown 5% Yb^{3+}:LuLiF$_4$ crystal of size 2 × 2 × 5 mm^3 is deduced from the LITMoS-measured cooling parameters. Corresponding results indicate that this crystal sample can be potentially cooled to about 110 K.

2. LITMoS Test Theory

The cooling efficiency $\eta_c(\lambda, T)$ is used to deduce the cooling grade of the material and expresses as [36]:

$$\eta_c(\lambda, T) = 1 - \eta_{ext} \frac{\alpha_r(\lambda, T)}{\alpha_r(\lambda, T) + \alpha_b} \frac{\lambda}{\lambda_f(T)} \quad (1)$$

where η_{ext} is the external quantum efficiency, and $\alpha_r(\lambda, T)$ and α_b are the resonance absorption coefficient and the background absorption coefficient, respectively. The four parameters $\eta_{ext}, \alpha_b, \lambda_f(T)$ and $\alpha_r(\lambda, T)$ in Equation (1) describe the optical cooling grade of the sample. It is necessary to precisely measure the four parameters above to calculate the wavelength- and temperature-dependent cooling efficiency contour map (cooling window).

The effect of various thermal loads on the sample can be expressed as:

$$C_v \frac{dT}{dt} = -\eta_c P_{abs} + \frac{\varepsilon_s A_s \sigma}{1+\chi}\left(T_a^4 - T_s^4\right) + A_s k_h (T_a - T_s) + \frac{N k_l A_l}{d_l}(T_a - T_s) \quad (2)$$

In the right side of the equation, the first term represents the heat extracted from the anti-Stokes cooling. The second term represents the radiative heat load from the ambience. The third and fourth terms represent the convective and conductive heat loads on the sample, respectively. $\sigma = 5.67 \times 10^{-8}$ W/mm^{2}K^4 is the Stefan-Boltzmann constant and $\chi = (1 - \varepsilon_a)\varepsilon_s A_s / \varepsilon_a A_a$. Here $T_{a,s}$, $A_{a,s}$ and $\varepsilon_{a,s}$ are the temperature, the surface area and the thermal emissivity, respectively. Subscripts a and s denote the ambience and the sample. N is the number of contacting points with the length d_l of support, the area A_l of the contact points and the conductivity k_l of support. k_h is the convective heat transfer coefficient of the surrounding. $C_v = c_v \rho V$ is the heat capacity, where ρ, c_v and V are specifically the heat, density and volume of the sample, respectively.

The last two terms in Equation (2) represent the convective heat load and the conductive heat load on the samples, respectively. Their contributions can be neglected for a sample supported by two optical fibers of 100 μm diameters inside the high vacuum cavity. Since the cavity surface area A_a is much larger than the sample surface area A_s, the influence of χ can be neglected. For the case of the small temperature change $\Delta T(T_a - T_s \leq 5\,\text{K})$, Equation (2) is simplified as [46].

$$C_v \frac{dT}{dt} \approx -\eta_c P_{abs} - 4\varepsilon_s A_s \sigma T_a^3 (T_s - T_a) \tag{3}$$

The experimentally measured cooling efficiency $\eta_c(\lambda)^{exp}$ under steady-state ($dT/dt = 0$) condition can be expressed as Equation (4).

$$\eta_c(\lambda)^{exp} = K_{rad} \cdot \Delta T / P_{abs}(\lambda) \tag{4}$$

where $K_{rad} = 4\varepsilon_s A_s \sigma T_a^3$ and $P_{abs}(\lambda) \propto k \int S(\lambda) d\lambda$. Here, k and $S(\lambda)$ are the scaling factor and the fluorescence spectrum, respectively. The cooling efficiency of the sample $\eta_c(\lambda)^{exp}$ can be obtained by precisely measuring the sample temperature change ΔT as a function of the pump wavelength λ and the absorption power. To accurately measure the laser-induced temperature change ΔT, a special experimental set-up has been designed to minimize the sample's external thermal load and a calibrated thermal imaging camera is used to precisely monitor the sample temperature in real time.

With the measured values of the average fluorescence wavelength of the sample $\lambda_f(T)$ and the resonance absorption coefficient $\alpha_r(\lambda, T)$, the external quantum efficiency η_{ext} and the background absorption coefficient α_b can be obtained by fitting the cooling efficiency $\eta_c(\lambda)^{exp}$ measured in the experiment utilizing Equation (1). Two zero-crossing wavelengths can be observed throughout the crystal temperature change. The external quantum efficiency η_{ext} is determined by the ratio of the average fluorescence wavelength λ_f to the first zero-crossing wavelength λ_{cross1} [46]. The second crossing wavelength λ_{cross2} helps solve the background absorption coefficient α_b on the basis of Equation (1) with the measured parameters of η_{ext}, $\lambda_f(T)$ and $\alpha_r(\lambda, T)$.

3. Experimental Set-Up

A schematic diagram of the experimental set-up for LITMoS testing is shown in Figure 1. A tunable fiber laser with a wavelength range of 1010–1080 nm is used to pump the 5% Yb^{3+}-doped LuLiF$_4$ crystal with size of 2 × 2 × 5 mm^3. The sample is placed in the vacuum chamber of 10^{-5} Pa. The pump laser beam is collected by beam dump after passing through the sample. A calibrated thermal camera (FLIR A300) equipped with 100 µm macro lens is used to measure the temperature change ΔT of the sample in real time. A spectrometer (Ocean Optics Maya 2000Pro-NIR, Dunedin, FL, USA) is used to measure the fluorescence spectra and the absorption power $P_{abs}(\lambda)$ of the sample. The cooling efficiency $\eta_c(\lambda)^{exp}$ of the sample at the different pump wavelength λ can be acquired by precisely measuring ΔT and $P_{abs}(\lambda)$.

Figure 2 shows the picture of devices for the LITMoS test and the thermal camera calibration. The picture of the thermal camera and the cooling grade testing chamber (CGTC) is shown in Figure 2a. The infrared camera is used for non-contact temperature measurement in the LITMoS test. The camera's detector contains a focal plane array of uncooled micro-radiometric thermometers (320 × 240 pixels) and a spectral response range of 7.5–13 µm. The BK7 glass windows (25 mm diameter) for pump laser are AR coated at a wavelength of 1 µm. The other pair of BaF$_2$ windows (25 mm diameter) is used for the sample temperature measurement with the thermal camera. The temperature of the CGTC can be adjusted in the range of 276–308 K with an accuracy of ±0.05 K by the chiller. The interior of the CGTC is shown in Figure 2b. There are two copper blocks with a slit in the middle for accommodating a reference sample identical in size to the cooling one. A TEC is contact-fixed to the copper clamp for varying the sample temperature. A K-type thermocouple with very thin strings is connected to the copper clamp for temperature measurement. A low-evaporation silicone grease is used on all contact surfaces for good thermal conductivity. These electronic devices are wired to the outside of the CGTC through connectors on the sealed cap. The temperature of the reference sample, which is embedded in the sample holder, can be controlled by adjusting the current of the TEC and measured by the thermal camera at the same time. Figure 2c shows the side view of the CGTC.

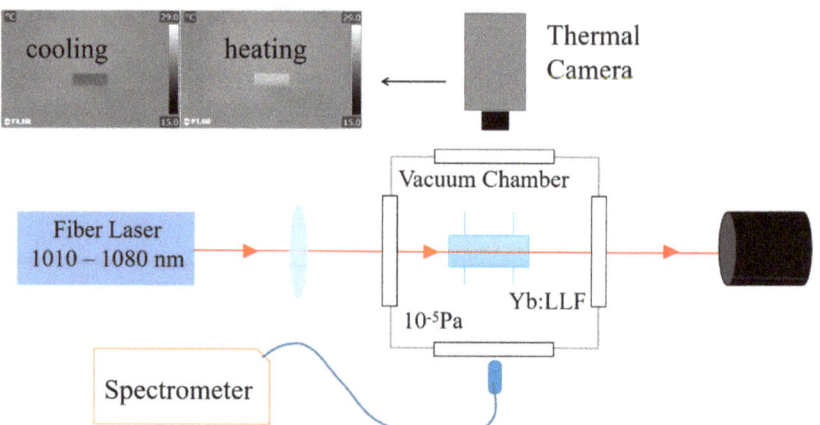

Figure 1. The schematic of the LITMoS test set-up.

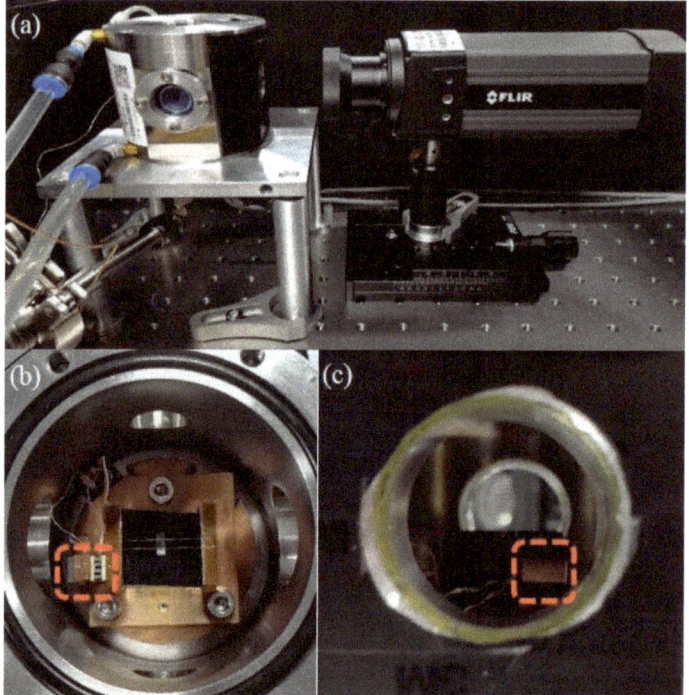

Figure 2. The photograph of the LITMoS test set-up and the thermal camera calibration. (**a**) The cooling grade testing chamber with the water chiller and the thermal camera (FIRE A300). (**b**) The interior of the cooling grade testing chamber (top view). The TEC and copper clam, including the reference sample (inside the area of the red dash box). (**c**) The interior of the cooling grade testing chamber (side view).

It is difficult to directly measure the temperature change of the sample in the CGTC using thermal camera imaging because the sample has low thermal emissivity and is transparent at thermal wavelengths. In order to identify the proportional relationship between pixel brightness and temperature change of the sample, it is necessary to vary the temperature of the sample inside the CGTC and acquire its thermal images accordingly. The micro-radiometer technology is based on the principle that the change in pixel resistivity is proportional to the energy of the infrared radiation absorbed by the detector. After calibration, one can deduce the temperature of the emitting source from the pixel intensity variation of the output images. The thermal camera outputs an 8-bit depth grayscale image with intensity values between 0 (black) and 255 (white) for each pixel in the photo. By calibrating the proportional relationship between pixel intensity and temperature, the change of the target temperature within the thermal image region can be inferred from the change of the pixel intensity. To measure the change in the sample temperature in real time, the thermal image of the sample is recorded for a sufficiently long time (30–50 min) while the ambient temperature is kept constant.

In order to minimize the fluctuations, the pixel intensity values of the specified area, as shown by the red dash line box in the thermal image in Figure 3a, are summed and averaged. It is important to specify the temperature scale range of the thermal image, such as 288–302 K for our case here, and establish the mapping relationship between temperature and pixel intensity. The pixel intensity at the lowest temperature of 288 K is 0, and the pixel intensity at the highest temperature of 302 K is 255. The dependence relationship of the reference sample temperature in the copper clamp on the TEC current is affected by both the background pressure of the vacuum and the temperature of the CGTC, as shown in Figure 3b. To minimize the effect of background pressure, the CGTC is maintained in a high vacuum of ~10^{-5} Pa during the whole process of the experiment.

The pixel intensities of the thermal image of the reference sample (LuLiF$_4$ crystal) are measured with the temperature of the surrounding CGTC being 295 K and 293 K, respectively. The temperature scale range of the thermal image is chosen from 288 K to 302 K, as shown in Figure 3c. The black and red dots correspond to results for the cases of the CGTC temperature being 295 K and 293 K, respectively. Although the slopes of the two fitting lines are almost the same, the absolute pixel intensities of the reference sample are different for the same sample temperature. Therefore, the temperature of the surrounding CGTC should be kept constant during the whole process of the LITMoS test.

Figure 3d shows the relationship between the measured pixel intensity variation Δpixel (Δpixel = P − P$_R$) of the thermal image and the temperature variation ΔT ($\Delta T = T - T_R$) of the sample. Here, P$_R$ indicates the pixel intensity of the thermal image at the reference temperature of T_R, which is the same as the surrounding CGTC temperature (295 K). The red dots correspond to the case with the temperature scale range of the thermal images being 288–302 K. The red solid line is a linear fit of the measured results. For $|\Delta T| \leq 5$ K, the relationship between Δpixel and ΔT is rather linear. As the value of $|\Delta T|$ grows, the relationship deviates more from being linear. Therefore, the variation of the sample temperature $|\Delta T|$ is kept at no more than 5 K in our LITMoS test. The slope of the linear fit, $\Delta T / \Delta$pixel, defines the calibration factor, which is 0.07736 for the case here and used for later determination of the sample temperature variation from the pixel intensity of the thermal image.

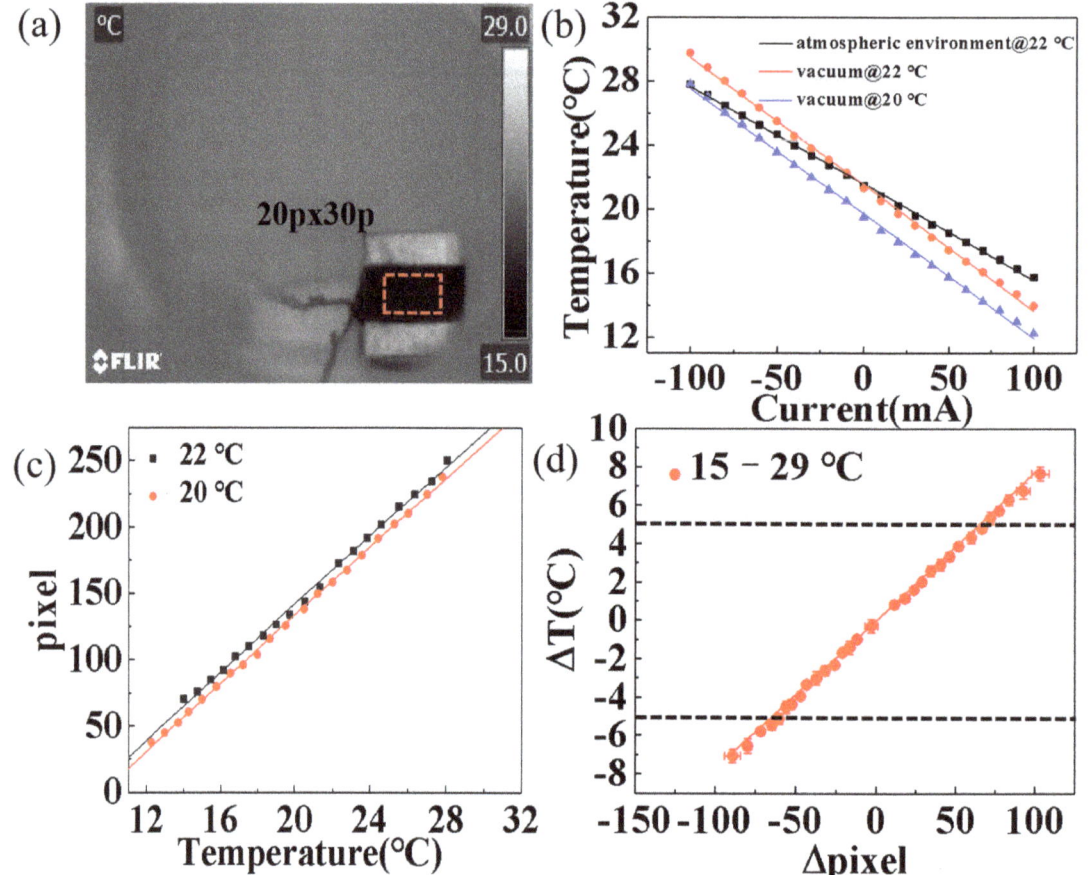

Figure 3. The calibration of the thermal camera. (**a**) The side view of the thermal image of the CGTC through the BaF$_2$ windows. The red dash area on the surface of the sample is used for calculating the average pixel intensity. (**b**) The variation in the reference crystal temperature with TEC current for three cases. (**c**) Calibrating the relationship between the pixel values of the sample thermal image and its temperature. (**d**) The relationship between the pixel value changes of the sample thermal image and its temperature.

4. Results and Discussions

Under the irradiation of the 1015 nm pump laser, the 5% Yb^{3+}-doped LuLiF$_4$ crystal is optically cooled. With the decrease in the sample temperature the pixel intensities of thermal images are reduced, as shown in Figure 4a. The sample temperature reaches a steady state after 20 min of irradiation. The averaged pixel intensities decrease from 158 to 102.1, corresponding to a pixel intensity drop of 55.9 and a sample temperature drop of about 4.3 K. When the pump wavelength is changed to 1080 nm, the 5% Yb^{3+}-doped LuLiF$_4$ crystal is optically heated. The sample reaches a steady state in temperature after 20 min of irradiation. With the increase in the sample temperature, the pixel intensities of thermal images are enhanced, as shown in Figure 4b. The averaged pixel intensities increase from 161.8 to 206, corresponding to a pixel intensity rise of 44.2 and a sample temperature rise of about 3.4 K.

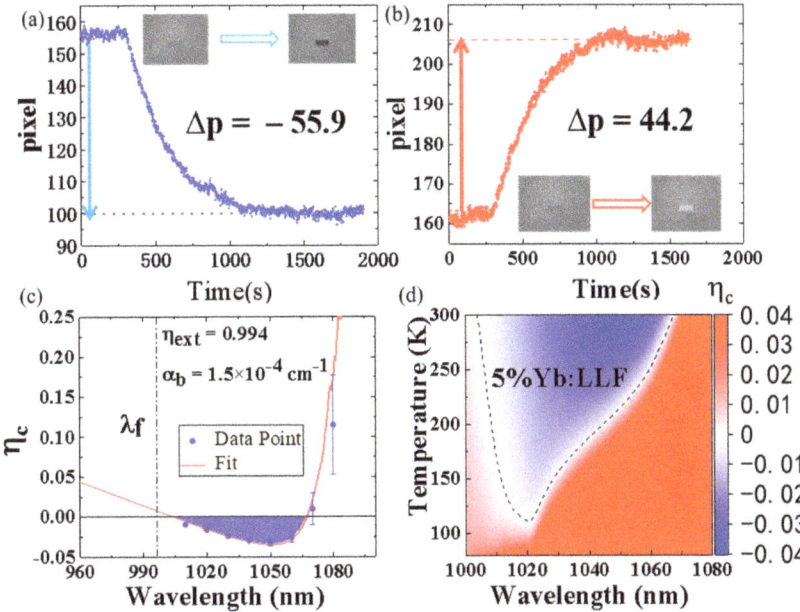

Figure 4. The LITMoS test of the 5% Yb^{3+}:LuLiF$_4$ crystal. (**a**) The pixel intensity changes of the thermal camera at 1015 nm pumping. The inset is the thermal image of the sample. (**b**) The pixel intensity changes of the thermal camera at 1080 nm pumping. The inset is the thermal image of the sample. (**c**) The measured $\eta_c(\lambda)^{exp}$ as shown by blue dots and model fitting of Equation (1) with the parameters of $\eta_{ext} = 99.4(\pm 0.1)\%$ and $\alpha_b = 1.5(\pm 0.1) \times 10^{-4}$ cm^{-1} as shown by the red solid curve. (**d**) The cooling window of 5% Yb^{3+}:LuLiF$_4$ crystal. The blue region and the red region correspond to cooling and heating, respectively.

Similar experimental studies were also performed in other pump wavelengths in the range of 1010 nm and 1080 nm. The temperature changes of the crystal at each pump wavelength were extracted from thermal images following the above-mentioned image-processing procedure, which involves both spatial and temporal averaging. The CGTC temperature was kept at a constant value of 22 °C during the experiment. The absorbed power $P_{abs}(\lambda) \propto k \int S(\lambda)d\lambda$ at each pump wavelength λ was calculated from the photoluminescence excitation spectroscopy measurement technique. The measured cooling efficiency $\eta_c(\lambda)^{exp}$ for each pump wavelength was fitted with Equation (1). The corresponding results are shown in Figure 4c. The external quantum efficiency $\eta_{ext} = 99.4(\pm 0.1)\%$ and the background absorption coefficient $\alpha_b = 1.5(\pm 0.1) \times 10^{-4}$ cm^{-1} are acquired accordingly. The net cooling of the sample is observed between the first zero-crossing wavelength λ_{cross1} = 1005 nm and the second crossing wavelength λ_{cross2} = 1065 nm. The filled blue region between λ_{cross1} and λ_{cross2} represents the cooling area.

A "cooling window" capable of predicting the optical cooling potential of the sample can be calculated according to the cooling parameters of the crystal, such as η_{ext}, α_b, α_r and λ_f measured in experiment. Figure 4d shows the "cooling window" of the 5% Yb^{3+}:LuLiF$_4$ crystal under our study. The dash line separating the blue area of cooling and red area of heating indicates the points where the cooling efficiency is equal to zero. From Figure 4d one can see that the global MAT of the crystal can reach ~110 K at 1020 nm by maximizing the power absorption of the pump laser (astigmatic Herriot cavity [55,56]) and minimizing heat loads from the environment [46,49,50].

The cooling performance of a sample strongly depends on its cooling parameters, such as η_{ext} and α_b etc. In a previous work, a temperature drop of ~2.2 K was reported in a

Czochralski-grown bulk 5% Yb^{3+}-doped $LuLiF_4$ under 1025 nm pump laser of 220 mW with the corresponding parameters $\eta_{ext} = 99.0\ (\pm 0.1)$, $\alpha_b = 1.3\ (\pm 0.2) \times 10^{-3}\ cm^{-1}$ [57]. Later a Czochralski-grown bulk 5% Yb^{3+}-doped $LuLiF_4$ of better purity was cooled to 117.3 K under 1020 nm pump laser of 33 W with estimated cooling parameters being $\eta_{ext} = 99.4\%$ and $\alpha_b = 4.5 \times 10^{-4}\ cm^{-1}$ [29] Recently, a Bridgman-grown 5% Yb^{3+}-doped $LuLiF_4$ was cooled to ~195 K under 1020 nm pump laser of 45 W with $\eta_{ext} = 98.9\ (\pm 0.1)\%$ and $\alpha_b = 3.3\ (\pm 0.2) \times 10^{-4}\ cm^{-1}$ [58]. Based on the cooling window from the LITMoS test, the crystal sample under current study can be potentially cooled to ~110 K under 1020 nm pump laser with its measured parameters $\eta_{ext} = 99.4\ (\pm 0.1)\%$ and $\alpha_b = 1.5\ (\pm 0.1) \times 10^{-4}\ cm^{-1}$ In a recent report working with 5% Yb, Tm co-doped $LiYF_4$ crystal, A. Volpi et al. found that when the sample temperature decreased from 300 K to 100 K, the corresponding background absorption α_b dropped more than an order of magnitude [41]. This study indicated that the background absorption α_b does not remain constant but changes dramatically during the cooling process. As an isomorph of the $LiYF_4$ crystal, the $LuLiF_4$ crystal displays similar optical behavior [57–60]. Considering the reduction in α_b with decreasing temperature [41], one can expect that the 5% Yb^{3+}:$LuLiF_4$ crystal under our study can be potentially cooled to even lower temperatures than 110 K.

5. Conclusions

The LITMoS test has been adopted here to measure the laser-cooling properties of the 5% Yb^{3+}:$LuLiF_4$ crystal placed inside a special cooling-grade test chamber at room temperature. With a carefully calibrated thermal camera (temperature resolution < 0.1 K), the external quantum efficiency η_{ext} and the background absorption coefficient α_b of the sample were accurately measured to be $\eta_{ext} = 99.4\ (\pm 0.1)\%$ and $\alpha_b = 1.5\ (\pm 0.1) \times 10^{-4}\ cm^{-1}$, respectively. The cooling window of the sample was deduced from the LITMoS measured parameters and indicates a global MAT of ~110 K. Our study shows that the 5% Yb^{3+}:$LuLiF_4$ crystal is of excellent laser-cooling grade for applications in cryogenic optical coolers and RBLs.

Author Contributions: Conceptualization, methodology, software, analysis, investigation, X.D., B.Z., Y.L., C.W., J.X., Z.Z., J.D. and J.Y.; Writing—original draft preparation, X.D.; writing—review and editing, B.Z.; visualization, supervision, B.Z. and J.Y. All authors have read and agreed to the published version of the manuscript.

Funding: This work is partially supported by the Fundamental Research Funds for the Central Universities, the National Natural Science Foundation of China (Grant Nos. 11604100, 11834003, 61574056, 91536218, and 11874151), the Special Financial Grant from the China Postdoctoral Science Foundation (Grant No. 2016T90346) and 111 Project (B12024).

Institutional Review Board Statement: Not applicable.

Informed Consent Statement: Not applicable.

Data Availability Statement: All data sets obtained in this research are available upon request.

Acknowledgments: We thank J.W. Meng for helpful discussion and assistance, and B. Zhong thanks L.Z. Deng for his generous help.

Conflicts of Interest: The authors declare no conflict of interest.

References

1. Epstein, R.I.; Buchwald, M.I.; Edwards, B.C.; Gosnell, T.R.; Mungan, C.E. Observation of laser-induced fluorescent cooling of a solid. *Nature* **1995**, *377*, 500–503. [CrossRef]
2. Seletskiy, D.V.; Melgaard, S.D.; Bigotta, S.; Di Lieto, A.; Tonelli, M.; Sheik-Bahae, M. Laser cooling of solids to cryogenic temperatures. *Nat. Photonics* **2010**, *4*, 161–164. [CrossRef]
3. Mills, G.; Mord, A. Performance modeling of optical refrigerators. *Cryogenics* **2006**, *46*, 176–182. [CrossRef]
4. Nemova, G.; Kashyap, R. Laser cooling of solids. *Rep. Prog. Phys.* **2010**, *73*, 086501. [CrossRef]
5. Nemova, G. *Laser Cooling: Fundamental Properties and Applications*; Jenny Stanford Publishing: New York, NY, USA, 2016.

6. Epstein, R.I.; Sheik-Bahae, M. *Optical Refrigeration: Science and Applications of Laser Cooling of Solids*; John Wiley & Sons: Hoboken, NJ, USA, 2010.
7. Seletskiy, D.; Hehlen, M.; Epstein, R.; Sheik-Bahae, M. Cryogenic optical refrigeration. *Adv. Opt. Photonics* **2012**, *4*, 78–107. [CrossRef]
8. Rostami, S.; Albrecht, A.R.; Volpi, A.; Hehlen, M.P.; Tonelli, M.; Sheik-Bahae, M. Tm-doped crystals for mid-IR optical cryocoolers and radiation balanced lasers. *Opt. Lett.* **2019**, *44*, 1419–1422. [CrossRef]
9. Yang, Z.; Meng, J.; Albrecht, A.R.; Sheik-Bahae, M. Radiation-balanced Yb:YAG disk laser. *Opt. Express* **2019**, *27*, 1392–1400. [CrossRef]
10. Xia, X.; Pant, A.; Davis, E.J.; Pauzauskie, P.J. Design of a radiation-balanced fiber laser via optically active composite cladding materials. *J. Opt. Soc. Am. B* **2019**, *36*, 3307–3314. [CrossRef]
11. Khurgin, J.B. Radiation-balanced tandem semiconductor/Yb3+:YLF lasers: Feasibility study. *J. Opt. Soc. Am. B* **2020**, *37*, 1886–1895. [CrossRef]
12. Knall, J.M.; Engholm, M.; Boilard, T.; Bernier, M.; Digonnet, M.J.F. Radiation-Balanced Silica Fiber Amplifier. *Phys. Rev. Lett.* **2021**, *127*, 013903. [CrossRef]
13. Nemova, G. Radiation-Balanced Lasers: History, Status, Potential. *Appl. Sci.* **2021**, *11*, 7539. [CrossRef]
14. Peysokhan, M.; Mobini, E.; Allahverdi, A.; Abaie, B.; Mafi, A. Characterization of Yb-doped ZBLAN fiber as a platform for radiation-balanced lasers. *Photon. Res.* **2020**, *8*, 202–210. [CrossRef]
15. Melgaard, S.; Seletskiy, D.; Polyak, V.; Asmerom, Y.; Sheik-Bahae, M. Identification of parasitic losses in Yb:YLF and prospects for optical refrigeration down to 80K. *Opt. Express* **2014**, *22*, 7756–7764. [CrossRef] [PubMed]
16. Hoyt, C.W.; Hasselbeck, M.P.; Sheik-Bahae, M.; Epstein, R.I.; Greenfield, S.; Thiede, J.; Distel, J.; Valencia, J. Advances in laser cooling of thulium-doped glass. *J. Opt. Soc. Am. B* **2003**, *20*, 1066–1074. [CrossRef]
17. Walsh, B.M.; Barnes, N.P.; Petros, M.; Yu, J.; Singh, U.N. Spectroscopy and modeling of solid state lanthanide lasers: Application to trivalent Tm^{3+} and Ho^{3+} in $YLiF_4$ and $LuLiF_4$. *J. Appl. Phys.* **2004**, *95*, 3255–3271. [CrossRef]
18. Rostami, S.; Albrecht, A.R.; Volpi, A.; Sheik-Bahae, M. Observation of optical refrigeration in a holmium-doped crystal. *Photonics Res.* **2019**, *7*, 445–450. [CrossRef]
19. Fernandez, J.; Garcia-Adeva, A.J.; Balda, R. Anti-stokes laser cooling in bulk erbium-doped materials. *Phys. Rev. Lett.* **2006**, *97*, 033001. [CrossRef]
20. Garcia-Adeva, A.J. Spectroscopy, upconversion dynamics, and applications of -doped low-phonon materials. *J. Lumin.* **2008**, *128*, 697–702. [CrossRef]
21. Nemova, G.; Kashyap, R. Laser cooling of Er^{3+}-doped solids. *Opt. Commun.* **2010**, *283*, 3736–3739. [CrossRef]
22. Soares de Lima Filho, E.; Nemova, G.; Loranger, S.; Kashyap, R. Laser-induced cooling of a Yb: YAG crystal in air at atmospheric pressure. *Opt. Express* **2013**, *21*, 24711–24720. [CrossRef]
23. Nemova, G.; Kashyap, R. Laser cooling in Yb^{3+}:YAG. *J. Opt. Soc. Am. B* **2014**, *31*, 340–348. [CrossRef]
24. Cante, S.; Valle, S.; Yoon, S.J.; Mackenzie, J.I. 60W 946nm cryogenically-cooled Nd: YAG laser. *Appl. Phys. B* **2019**, *125*, 135–141. [CrossRef]
25. Allison, S.W.; Beshears, D.L.; Cates, M.R.; Scudiere, M.B.; Shaw, D.W.; Ellis, A.D. Luminescence of YAG: Dy and YAG: Dy, Er crystals to 1700 °C. *Meas. Sci. Technol.* **2020**, *31*, 1–10. [CrossRef]
26. Zhong, B.; Yin, J.; Jia, Y.; Chen, L.; Hang, Y.; Yin, J. Laser cooling of Yb^{3+}-doped $LuLiF_4$ crystal. *Opt. Lett.* **2014**, *39*, 2747–2750. [CrossRef] [PubMed]
27. Zhong, B.; Luo, H.; Shi, Y.; Yin, J. Laser cooling of 5 mol. % Yb^{3+}:$LuLiF_4$ crystal in air. *Opt. Eng.* **2016**, *56*, 011102. [CrossRef]
28. Zhong, B.; Luo, H.; Lei, Y.; Shi, Y.; Yin, J. *Forward to Cryogenic Temperature: Laser Cooling of Yb:LuLiF Crystal*; Society of Photo-Optical Instrumentation Engineers (SPIE) Conference Series: San Francisco, CA, USA, 2017; p. 101800C.
29. Zhong, B.; Lei, Y.; Luo, H.; Shi, Y.; Yang, T.; Yin, J. Laser cooling of the Yb^{3+}-doped $LuLiF_4$ single crystal for optical refrigeration. *J. Lumin.* **2020**, *226*, 117472. [CrossRef]
30. Püschel, S.; Mauerhoff, F.; Kränkel, C.; Tanaka, H. Solid-state laser cooling in Yb:CaF_2 and Yb:SrF^2 by anti-Stokes fluorescence. *Opt. Lett.* **2022**, *47*, 333–336. [CrossRef]
31. Zhong, B.; Lei, Y.; Duan, X.; Yang, T.; Yin, J. Optical refrigeration of the Yb^{3+}-doped YAG crystal close to the thermoelectric cooling limit. *Appl. Phys. Lett.* **2021**, *118*, 131104. [CrossRef]
32. Hehlen, M.; Epstein, R.; Inoue, H. Model of Laser Cooling in the Yb^{3+}-Doped Fluorozirconate Glass ZBLAN. *Phys. Rev. B* **2007**, *75*, 144302. [CrossRef]
33. Thiede, J.; Distel, J.; Greenfield, S.R.; Epstein, R.I. Cooling to 208 K by optical refrigeration. *Appl. Phys. Lett.* **2005**, *86*, 154107. [CrossRef]
34. Thomas, J.; Meyneng, T.; Ledemi, Y.; Rakotonandrasana, A.; Seletskiy, D.; Maia, L.; Messaddeq, Y.; Kashyap, R.; Epstein, R.I.; Seletskiy, D.V.; et al. *Oxyfluoride Glass-Ceramics: A Bright Future for Laser Cooling*; Photonic Heat Engines: Science and Applications II; SPIE OPTO: San Francisco, CA, USA, 2020; p. 112980E.
35. Ruan, X.L.; Kaviany, M. Advances in Laser Cooling of Solids. *J. Heat Transfer* **2006**, *129*, 3–8. [CrossRef]
36. Sheik-Bahae, M.; Epstein, R.I. Optical refrigeration. *Nat. Photonics* **2007**, *1*, 693–699. [CrossRef]
37. Seletskiy, D.V.; Melgaard, S.D.; Lieto, A.D.; Tonelli, M.; Sheikbahae, M. Laser cooling of a semiconductor load to 165 K. *Opt. Express* **2010**, *18*, 18061–18066. [CrossRef]

38. Hehlen, M.P.; Sheik-Bahae, M.; Epstein, R.I.; Melgaard, S.D.; Seletskiy, D.V. Materials for Optical Cryocoolers. *J. Mater. Chem.* **2013**, *1*, 1–8. [CrossRef]
39. Xia, X.; Pant, A.; Ganas, A.S.; Jelezko, F.; Pauzauskie, P.J. Quantum Point Defects for Solid-State Laser Refrigeration. *Adv. Mater.* **2021**, *33*, 1905406. [CrossRef]
40. Bigotta, S.; Di Lieto, A.; Parisi, D.; Toncelli, A.; Tonelli, M. *Single Fluoride Crystals as Materials for Laser Cooling Applications*; Laser Cooling of Solids: San Jose, CA, USA, 2007; pp. 75–84.
41. Volpi, A.; Meng, J.; Gragossian, A.; Albrecht, A.R.; Rostami, S.; Lieto, A.D.; Epstein, R.I.; Tonelli, M.; Hehlen, M.P.; Sheik-Bahae, M. Optical refrigeration: The role of parasitic absorption at cryogenic temperatures. *Opt. Express* **2019**, *27*, 29710–29718. [CrossRef]
42. Peysokhan, M.; Rostami, S.; Mobini, E.; Albrecht, A.R.; Kuhn, S.; Hein, S.; Hupel, C.; Nold, J.; Haarlammert, N.; Schreiber, T.; et al. Implementation of Laser-Induced Anti-Stokes Fluorescence Power Cooling of Ytterbium-Doped Silica Glass. *ACS Omega* **2021**, *6*, 8376–8381. [CrossRef]
43. Knall, J.; Engholm, M.; Ballato, J.; Dragic, P.D.; Yu, N.; Digonnet, M.J. Experimental comparison of silica fibers for laser cooling. *Opt. Lett.* **2020**, *45*, 4020–4023. [CrossRef]
44. Knall, J.; Engholm, M.; Boilard, T.; Bernier, M.; Vigneron, P.B.; Yu, N.; Dragic, P.D.; Ballato, J.; Digonnet, M.J.F. Radiation-balanced silica fiber laser. *Optica* **2021**, *8*, 830–833. [CrossRef]
45. Knall, J.; Digonnet, M. Design of High-Power Radiation-Balanced Silica Fiber Lasers with a Doped Core and Cladding. *J. Lightwave Technol.* **2021**, *39*, 2497–2504. [CrossRef]
46. Melgaard, S.D. Cryogenic Optical Refrigeration: Laser Cooling of Solids Below 123 K. Ph.D. Thesis, University of New Mexico, Albuquerque, NM, USA, 2013.
47. Volpi, A.; Kock, J.; Albrecht, A.R.; Hehlen, M.P.; Epstein, R.I.; Sheik-Bahae, M. Open-aperture Z-scan study for absorption saturation: Accurate measurement of saturation intensity in YLF: Yb for optical refrigeration. *Opt. Lett.* **2021**, *46*, 1421–1424. [CrossRef]
48. Seletskiy, D.V.; Melgaard, S.D.; Epstein, R.I.; Di Lieto, A.; Tonelli, M.; Sheik-Bahae, M. Precise determination of minimum achievable temperature for solid-state optical refrigeration. *J. Lumin.* **2013**, *133*, 5–9. [CrossRef]
49. Melgaard, S.D.; Seletskiy, D.V.; Di Lieto, A.; Tonelli, M.; Sheik-Bahae, M. Optical refrigeration to 119 K, below National Institute of Standards and Technology cryogenic temperature. *Opt. Lett.* **2013**, *38*, 1588–1590. [CrossRef]
50. Melgaard, S.D.; Albrecht, A.R.; Hehlen, M.P.; Sheik-Bahae, M. Solid-state optical refrigeration to sub-100 Kelvin regime. *Sci. Rep.* **2016**, *6*, 1–6. [CrossRef]
51. Gragossian, A.; Ghasemkhani, M.; Meng, J.; Albrecht, A.; Tonelli, M.; Sheik-Bahae, M. Optical refrigeration inches toward liquid-nitrogen temperatures. *SPIE Newsroom* **2017**, 2–4. [CrossRef]
52. Püschel, S.; Kalusniak, S.; Kränkel, C.; Tanaka, H. Temperature-dependent radiative lifetime of Yb: YLF: Refined cross sections and potential for laser cooling. *Opt. Express* **2021**, *29*, 11106–11120. [CrossRef]
53. Hehlen, M.P.; Meng, J.W.; Albrecht, A.R.; Lee, E.R.; Gragossian, A.; Love, S.P.; Hamilton, C.E.; Epstein, R.I.; Sheik-Bahae, M. First demonstration of an all-solid-state optical cryocooler. *Light Sci. Appl.* **2018**, *7*, 1–10. [CrossRef]
54. Volpi, A.; Di Lieto, A.; Tonelli, M. Novel approach for solid state cryocoolers. *Opt. Express* **2015**, *23*, 821626. [CrossRef]
55. Seletskiy, D.V.; Hasselbeck, M.P.; Sheik-Bahae, M. Resonant cavity-enhanced absorption for optical refrigeration. *Appl. Phys. Lett.* **2010**, *96*, 181106. [CrossRef]
56. Gragossian, A.; Meng, J.; Ghasemkhani, M.; Albrecht, A.R.; Sheik-Bahae, M. Astigmatic Herriott cell for optical refrigeration. *Opt. Eng.* **2016**, *56*, 011110. [CrossRef]
57. Volpi, A.; Cittadino, G.; Di Lieto, A.; Cassanho, A.; Jenssen, H.P.; Tonelli, M. Investigation of Yb-doped LiLuF^4 single crystals for optical cooling. *Opt. Eng.* **2016**, *56*, 011105. [CrossRef]
58. Volpi, A.; Krämer, K.W.; Biner, D.; Wiggins, B.; Kock, J.; Albrecht, A.R.; Peterson, E.J.; Spilde, M.N.; Sheik-Bahae, M.; Hehlen, M.P. Bridgman Growth of Laser-Cooling-Grade LiLuF4: Yb^{3+} Single Crystals. *Cryst. Growth Des.* **2021**, *21*, 2142–2153. [CrossRef]
59. Volpi, A. Laser Cooling of Fluoride Crystals. Ph.D. Thesis, University of Pisa, Pisa, Italy, 2012–2015.
60. Dobretsova, E.A.; Xia, X.; Pant, A.; Lim, M.B.; De Siena, M.C.; Boldyrev, K.N.; Molchanova, A.D.; Novikova, N.N.; Klimin, S.A.; Popova, M.N. Hydrothermal Synthesis of Yb^{3+}:LuLiF$_4$ Microcrystals and Laser Refrigeration of Yb^{3+}:LuLiF$_4$/Silicon-Nitride Composite Nanostructures. *Laser Photonics Rev.* **2021**, *15*, 2100019. [CrossRef]

Saturation, Allowed Transitions and Quantum Interference in Laser Cooling of Solids

Laura B. Andre [1,*], Long Cheng [1] and Stephen C. Rand [1,2]

[1] EECS Department, University of Michigan, Ann Arbor, MI 48109, USA; lonche@umich.edu (L.C.); scr@umich.edu (S.C.R.)
[2] Department of Physics, University of Michigan, Ann Arbor, MI 48109, USA
* Correspondence: lbandre@umich.edu

Abstract: New methods for the rapid cooling of solids with increased efficiency are analyzed and demonstrated experimentally. The advances offered by optical saturation, dipole-allowed transitions, and quantum interference for improved laser cooling of solids are highlighted.

Keywords: optical refrigeration; anti-Stokes fluorescence; absorption saturation; discrete resonances; lasing without inversion; Raman cooling

1. Introduction

Optical refrigeration was first achieved using laser-induced anti-Stokes fluorescent (ASF) emission in Yb^{3+}:ZBLANP glass in 1995 [1]. Since then, advances in experimental methods and the purification of materials have led to the optical cooling of numerous crystals [2], the reduction of attainable temperatures to the cryogenic range [3], the first optical cryocooler [4], and self-cooling or radiation-balanced lasers (RBLs) [5–7]. However, unintended impurities incorporated during sample preparation are still a key limitation to applications of ASF cooling [8]. Saturation of the absorption and reduction in the associated heating caused by background impurities can overcome this limitation under certain conditions. Hence, it is important to understand and characterize such nonlinear effects. In this study, the enhancement of laser cooling due to differential absorption saturation is analyzed and observed by two experimental methods. We also note that the cooling rate is limited by the excited state emission rate of coolant ions as the excited state lifetime determines the number of absorption/emission cycles each ion can undergo per unit time during ASF cooling. Electric-dipole-allowed (ED) transitions have very short upper state lifetimes; so, they can be cycled more rapidly for faster cooling. However, allowed transitions suffer from configuration relaxation and often mediate excited state absorption, both of which contribute to the internal heating of the sample. Consequently, while laser cooling on such transitions has been investigated previously [9], net cooling by this approach has not been reported until now. Finally, quantum interference has not been investigated for possible applications in laser cooling. In this paper, Fano resonance and induced transparency are analyzed for their potential to mediate self-cooled lasing without inversion in a 3-level system with two allowed transitions, modeled after trivalent Cerium.

Several advances are discussed here that enable cooling to lower minimum temperatures or more rapid cooling than has been possible to date with optical refrigeration based on anti-Stokes fluorescence (ASF). The first topic to be analyzed is optical saturation, relevant to attaining lower minimum temperatures by ASF cooling. As the laser cooling of solids is the only known method for refrigeration in space below the thermo-electric limit, any improvements in its capabilities will be important for future technology. Increased cooling efficiency through saturation is also demonstrated experimentally in Yb:LiYF$_3$ near room temperature. Optical refrigeration of Ti:Al$_2$O$_3$ on the allowed ^2E-$^2T_2$ transition is realized for the first time in a crystal with an exceptionally high figure of merit. This

result demonstrates that cooling on electric-dipole transitions is possible in a bulk solid and should enable more rapid cooling than can be achieved with ASF cooling on forbidden transitions of rare-earth ions. This advance should facilitate the development of imaging arrays with an improved signal-to-noise performance at cryogenic temperatures for sensing applications in outer space. In addition, it should encourage the development of new methods of cooling solids, such as Raman cooling. Analysis of the potential role of quantum interference in self-cooled lasers is also presented. Specific conditions are identified to enable self-cooled lasing without inversion in a Ce:LiCaAlF$_6$ laser.

2. Theory

In prior experimental research, the forbidden transitions of trivalent rare-earth ions such as Yb^{3+} were employed to demonstrate ASF cooling in insulating crystals and glasses While many proposals have been advanced to diversify the possible approaches for cooling and to extend the results to a wider class of materials [10–16], no alternatives to net cooling by anti-Stokes fluorescence have emerged. This failure has impeded the application of laser cooling to the refrigeration of semiconductor circuitry for sensors in space, although an ASF cryocooler for this type of application has been reported [4]. Better speed and efficiency of cooling would be highly advantageous for practical applications. In the following subsections, theoretical advances are described that address the need for the improved performance of optical refrigeration based on anti-Stokes fluorescence cooling through optical saturation and the use of electric-dipole-allowed transitions. The experimental realizations of these proposals are presented in Section 3.

2.1. Improved Cooling Efficiency Using Optical Saturation

The intensity dependence of the absorption coefficients of cooling ions and background impurities can be exploited to improve the cooling efficiency of ASF cooling. The following analysis of differential absorption saturation reveals its impact on laser cooling efficiency when background impurities saturate more easily than cooling ions.

The coolant ions and the background impurities are modeled as 2-level systems [13], with N_1, N_1' representing the number of ground state ions and impurities per unit volume. N_2, N_2' represent the density of the excited state species, respectively. Absent any internal laser field, the rate equation for the upper state population of the coolant ions is

$$\frac{dN_2}{dt} = \frac{I_p \lambda_p}{hc} \cdot [\sigma_a(\lambda_p, T) N_1 - \sigma_e(\lambda_p, T) N_2] - \frac{N_2}{\tau_f}. \quad (1)$$

For unintended impurities, it is

$$\frac{dN_2'}{dt} = \frac{\sigma' I_p \lambda_p}{hc} \cdot [N_1' - N_2'] - \frac{N_2'}{\tau'}. \quad (2)$$

I_p and λ_p denote the intensity and wavelength of the pump light. σ_a and σ_a are cross-sections for absorption and emission. τ_f and τ' are the excited state decay times of the coolant and impurity ions. In this model, the equation for heating power per unit volume is simply

$$H = I_p [\sigma_a(\lambda_p, T) N_1 - \sigma_e(\lambda_p, T) N_2] - \eta_e \frac{hc}{\lambda_f} \frac{N_2}{\tau_r} + \sigma' I_p [N_1' - N_2']. \quad (3)$$

Because there is no internal laser field to consider in refrigeration with a single pump beam, the population differences for the system under continuous illumination are given by the steady-state solutions of Equations (1) and (2). These expressions are

$$\Delta N \equiv N_1 - N_2 = \frac{N_T}{\frac{I_p}{I_{sat}} + 1} \quad (4)$$

and
$$\Delta N' \equiv N'_1 - N'_2 = \frac{N'_T}{\frac{I_p}{I'_{sat}} + 1}. \tag{5}$$

In these expressions, we have defined the saturation intensities [17] for the coolant and impurity ions, given by

$$I_{sat} = \frac{hc}{\lambda_p \tau_f [\sigma_a(\lambda_p, T) + \sigma_e(\lambda_p, T)]} \text{ and } I'_{sat} = \frac{hc}{2\sigma' \tau' \lambda_p}.$$

The total numbers of coolant and impurity species per unit volume are

$$N_T = N_1 + N_2 \tag{6}$$

and

$$N'_T = N'_1 + N'_2. \tag{7}$$

The steady-state heating power/volume obtained from Equation (3) is

$$H = I_p [\sigma_a(\lambda_p, T) \Delta N + \sigma' \Delta N'] \cdot \left[1 - \frac{\sigma_a(\lambda_p, T) \Delta N}{\sigma_a(\lambda_p, T) \Delta N + \sigma' \Delta N'} \eta_{ext} \frac{\lambda_p}{\lambda_f} \right]. \tag{8}$$

The final expression for cooling power in the presence of the optical saturation of the active ions and background impurities is therefore

$$P_c = -P_{abs} \left[1 - \frac{\sigma_a(\lambda_p, T) \Delta N}{\sigma_a(\lambda_p, T) \Delta N + \sigma' \Delta N'} \eta_{ext} \frac{\lambda_p}{\lambda_f} \right]. \tag{9}$$

The cooling efficiency η_c may be derived from Equation (9) as the ratio of the cooling power, P_c, to absorbed power, P_{abs}. This yields

$$\eta_c = \frac{P_c}{P_{abs}} = \eta_{ext} \frac{\lambda}{\lambda_f} \left[\frac{1}{1 + \alpha_b(I)/\alpha_r(I)} \right] - 1. \tag{10}$$

Here, the external quantum efficiency η_{ext} is the product of the fluorescence escape efficiency η_e and the internal quantum efficiency η_{QE} given by the ratio of the fluorescence and radiative lifetimes of the upper state. λ and I are the wavelength and intensity of the pump laser. The polarization-averaged mean fluorescence wavelength λ_f is determined from emission spectra. The absorption coefficients of the coolant ions, α_r, and background impurities, α_b, were assumed to be intensity-dependent. The form of this dependence [17] was taken to be $\alpha(I) = \alpha(0)/(1 + I/I_{sat})$, where the saturation intensity I_{sat} was assigned the values I_r or I_b for the coolant or background impurity ions, respectively.

The saturation intensity of the coolant ions varies with wavelength through its dependence on absorption and emission cross-sections. It is defined by the expression

$$I_r = \frac{hc}{\lambda \tau_f [\sigma_a(\lambda) + \sigma_e(\lambda)]}, \tag{11}$$

where τ_f is the fluorescence lifetime. The effective absorption cross-section $\sigma_a(\lambda)$ was measured directly with a spectrophotometer (SHIMADZU UV-3600) and corrected for instrument response. The effective emission cross-section $\sigma_e(\lambda)$ was then calculated using the McCumber relation [18]. This procedure ensured that the multiple Stark levels of Yb^{3+} and the Boltzmann population distribution among them were taken into account. Figure 1 displays the effective absorption and emission cross-sections of the 10% Yb:YLF crystal studied in our experiments and shows the position of the polarization-averaged mean fluorescence wavelength at 997.6 nm. Based on these cross-sections and a literature value for the Yb^{3+} fluorescence lifetime of 2.2 ms [19], the theoretical saturation intensity of the Yb^{3+} coolant ions was determined using Equation (11) and plotted as the continuous curve in Figure 2 versus wavelength. Surmising that an impurity such as Fe^{3+} is the main source of background absorption [9] and that it has a broadband spectrum centered around 1 micron [20], the saturation intensity I_b of the background may be presumed to be only weakly dependent on wavelength over the range of our experiments. With this one assumption, the experimental value of I_b can be estimated using the empirical approach outlined next and illustrated as a dashed line in Figure 2.

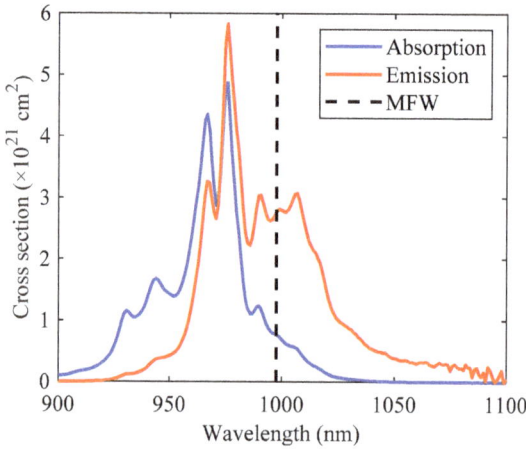

Figure 1. Absorption and emission cross-sections plot for E||c in 10% Yb^{3+}:$LiYF_4$. The blue curve is the effective absorption cross-section measured by a spectrophotometer, and the red is the effective emission cross-section calculated using the McCumber theory. The dashed vertical line indicates the polarization averaged mean fluorescence wavelength, 997.6 nm.

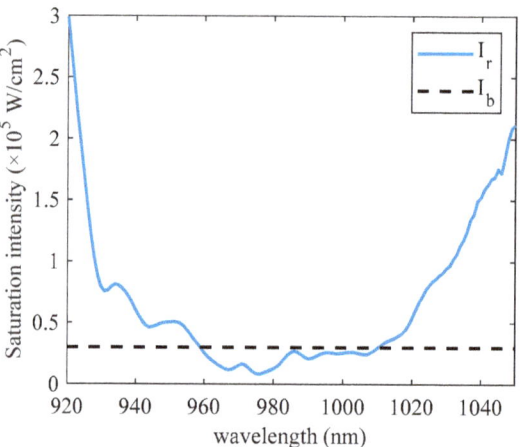

Figure 2. Theoretical saturation intensities versus wavelength. The blue curve shows the wavelength-dependent saturation intensity I_r of Yb^{3+} (from Equation (11)). The dashed line shows an arbitrary, constant saturation intensity level I_b of the background impurities. The plot illustrates an intersection point at $\lambda_{cr} = 1010$ nm on the low energy side of the Yb^{3+} absorption band, where $I_b = I_r(\lambda_{cr}) = 3 \times 10^4$ W/cm^2. The experimental determination of I_b, the intersection at λ_{cr} is determined by the wavelength where cooling efficiency curves recorded at different intensities intersect. At λ_{cr}, the wavelength-dependent saturation intensities are equal.

Figure 3 presents a theoretical plot of the cooling efficiencies given by Equation (10) at two pump intensities, namely $I = 3 \times 10^2$ W/cm^2 and $I = 3 \times 10^4$ W/cm^2. The first thing to notice is that at long wavelengths (>1 µm), the cooling efficiency increases at the higher pump intensity because the background impurities are easier to saturate than Yb^{3+} near their own broad resonance. Such long wavelengths are highly detuned from the absorption peak of Yb^{3+} (Figure 2). Naturally, saturation of the background reduces parasitic heating, leading to a significantly higher cooling efficiency in the long wavelength range. Closer to the absorption resonances of Yb^{3+}, at wavelengths of less than ~1 µm, the saturation intensity of the coolant ions drops, falling to a value below that of the background because the detuning is small. This raises the heat load and lowers the cooling efficiency at short wavelengths. Between these opposing trends, there is an intersection point in the plots versus wavelength of the saturation intensities (Figure 2) on the "red" side of the Yb^{3+} absorption band. The same is true of the intensity-dependent cooling efficiency plot (Figure 3). In Figure 3, this crossing point can be seen around 1010 nm, identifying a wavelength λ_{cr}, where the saturation intensities of the coolant ion and the background impurities are equal. The efficiency curves for all the input intensities cross at λ_{cr}, so the cooling efficiency is intensity-independent there. As the experimental saturation intensity of the background impurities equals that of Yb^{3+} at λ_{cr}, it can be determined by inserting λ_{cr} into Equation (11), yielding the result $I_b = I_r(\lambda_{cr})$.

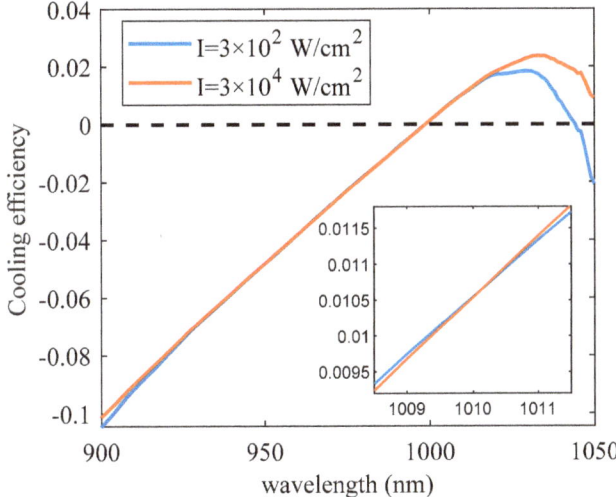

Figure 3. Theoretical cooling efficiency plotted using Equation (10) for two different pump intensities. The red and blue curves are the cooling efficiencies predicted at high and low intensity, respectively. For an arbitrary background saturation intensity of 3×10^4 W/cm^2, note that the high intensity curve intersects the low intensity one at 1010 nm, and the cooling efficiency grows to exceed its low intensity value at long wavelengths in the cooling range. For both plots, the absorption coefficient of background impurities was taken to be 1×10^{-3} cm^{-1} and the external quantum efficiency was unity.

2.2. Electric-Dipole-Allowed Transitions for Rapid Cooling

The efficiency of laser cooling by the ASF method is independent of the transition rate of the coolant atoms. This is clear because the upper state lifetime of these atoms is absent from Equation (10). On the other hand, the number of transitions per unit time does determine the speed of cooling. Hence, the transition rate of coolant atoms has an important impact on how quickly bulk systems can be cooled with light. This is confirmed in the expression for heating power density H, where the cooling term (second term on the right side of Equation (3) depends on the upper state radiative lifetime τ_r. From this equation, it is evident that the net heating or cooling power varies with the transition rate of the coolant atoms and improves significantly when the radiative lifetime on allowed transitions is short. Another way to think about the cooling term is that N_2/τ_r is proportional to the absorption cross-section. A medium 2, therefore, improves on the cooling power density of a medium 1 by the factor $\tau_{r1}/\tau_{r2} = \sigma_2/\sigma_1$, making it advantageous to use electric-dipole-allowed transitions for laser cooling, rather than forbidden transitions, because of their larger cross-sections. As most ED transitions have upper state decay times of less than 100 ns and forbidden transitions have lifetimes of ~1 ms, the cooling power can theoretically be increased by a factor of roughly 10^4 by using allowed transitions. Thus, this could result in a substantial improvement of the cool-down times.

Despite the high transition rate afforded by dipole-allowed transitions in solids, they normally incur heating due to non-radiative configuration relaxation. The mechanism is illustrated in Figure 4. The polarizability of excited state orbitals on allowed transitions in solids is susceptible to interactions with neighboring atoms. This shifts the minimum of the excited state potential to a greater distance from the nucleus than that of the ground state. According to the Franck–Condon principle, the absorption transition takes place rapidly enough so that the configuration coordinate Q does not change. Thus, the electron undergoes a vertical transition in Figure 4. which places it far from the equilibrium point at the bottom of the excited state well. This necessitates relaxation to the potential minimum, which is shifted to a larger value of the configuration coordinate Q. This relaxation, and a similar one that follows the vertical radiative transition to the ground state potential, is mediated by the emission of the vibrational quanta of the atomic cluster, consisting of the atom itself together with its neighbors in its coordination sphere. Fortunately, the emission of phonons and consequent heating that takes place during configuration relaxation can be mitigated to achieve net cooling in the same way as for systems with forbidden transitions, such as Yb^{3+}. Theoretically, one simply tunes the pump wavelength to a value exceeding the average Stokes-shifted emission wavelength of the coolant species. In Section 3.2, this strategy is shown to work on an ED transition in $Ti^{3+}:Al_2O_3$.

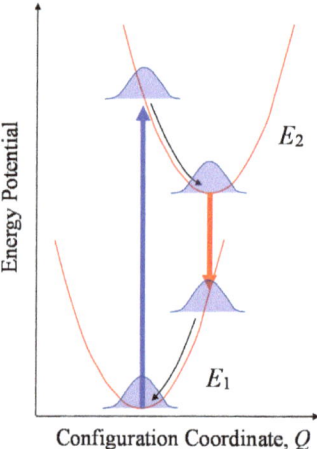

Figure 4. Potential energy curves for the ground state (E_1) and the excited state (E_2) of an atom in a solid. The vertical blue and red arrows depict fast dipole-allowed transitions upward to E_2 and downward to E_1, respectively, followed by configuration relaxation (black arrows). Because optical transitions take place vertically according to the Franck–Condon Principle, the system is pushed far from equilibrium. The difference in energy between the absorption and emission transitions, known as the Stokes shift, is particularly large in systems that undergo configuration relaxation. The relaxation process is mediated by phonon emission, which causes heating. The Gaussian-shaped curves illustrate the distribution of energy due to the optical interaction.

In the context of laser cooling, one thing which differentiates optical from acoustic phonons is their higher frequency and the limited number of allowed modes determined by crystal symmetry. Transitions involving optical modes have narrow linewidths and are well-defined in frequency. Hence, they exhibit quantum effects more readily than acoustic modes, which have a continuous density of states versus frequency. One consequence of this is illustrated in Figure 5, where the red arrow indicates excitation from the lowest sub-level of a vibrational ladder in the ground state (v = 1) to the lowest sub-level of the excited state (v' = 0).

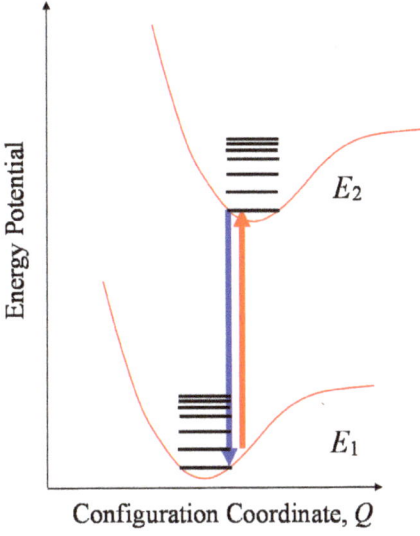

Figure 5. Quantized anti-Stokes luminescence in a 2-level system with electric-dipole-allowed transitions between ground and excited state vibrational sub-levels. The red arrow is a v = 1 to v' = 0 absorption transition. The blue arrow is a v' = 0 to v = 0 emission transition that contributes to cooling by avoiding configuration relaxation.

Such a transition avoids configuration relaxation because it takes place at a wavelength longer than the mean fluorescence wavelength. When this is the case, the quanta of the incident field have less energy than required to generate both the electronic transition and a phonon. Absorption is followed by anti-Stokes emission, shown as the downward blue arrow connecting v' = 0 to v = 0. The red and blue transitions jointly remove a vibrational quantum of the mode in question, thereby contributing to refrigeration. Other quantized absorption transitions are possible at longer wavelengths from the occupied sub-levels of other modes and other electronic sub-levels of the ground state. Figure 6 depicts a more detailed picture of the vibrational and electronic sub-levels of the $^2T_2$ ground state of $Ti^{3+}:Al_2O_3$ [21,22].

The absorptive transitions that contribute to cooling were all assumed to terminate in the lowest v' = 0 sub-level of the electronic excited state. This is necessary to avoid the generation of optical phonons. Because of the common final state, the cooling resonances are distinguishable by their initial states alone and form a discrete spectrum as a function of wavelength because all the electronic and optical mode energies exceed ~400 cm^{-1} and have low damping parameters [21].

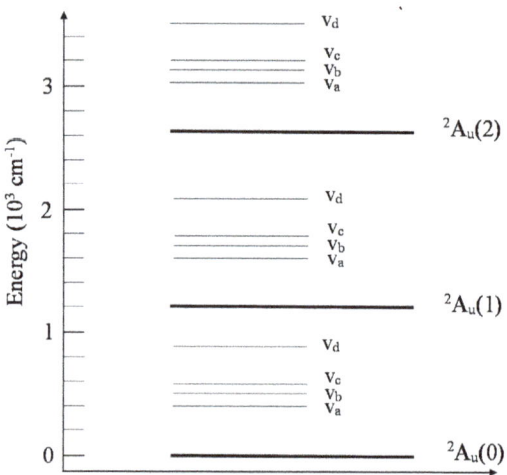

Figure 6. Energies of the sub-levels of the ground state of Ti:Al$_2$O$_3$ (to scale). The three ^2A_u electronic levels are labeled 0, 1, 2 in order of increasing energy, following Ref. [22]. The four vibrational sub-levels labeled a, b, c, d correspond to four allowed modes for π-polarization [21]. Only singly excited vibrational sub-levels are shown for each mode in association with each electronic state as only the first vibrational level is significantly populated at room temperature.

2.3. Quantum Interference for Self-Cooled Lasing without Inversion

In this section, Fano resonance mediated by excited state mixing and electromagnetically induced transparency (without any state mixing) are investigated in the system depicted in Figure 7, modeled after Ce^{3+} ions in the host crystal LiCaAlF$_6$. The Ce^{3+} dopant ions are characterized by having two allowed transitions, from states 1 to 2 and from 2 to 3. These are located in the ultraviolet spectral region. The transition from 1 to 3 is assumed to be forbidden by the usual rule of Laporte, and the lifetime of state 3 is correspondingly long.

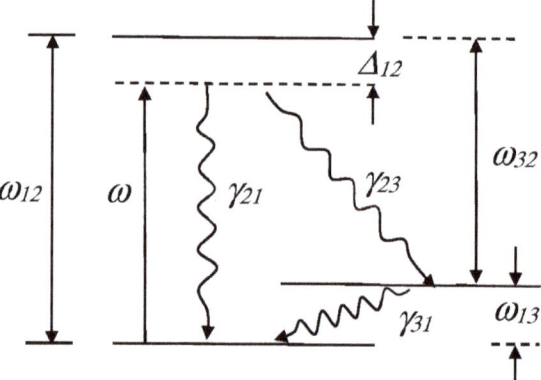

Figure 7. 3-level system with dipole-allowed transitions between states 1 and 2 and between states 2 and 3. State 3 is assumed to be metastable. The frequency of incident light is ω.

Two types of quantum interference can manifest themselves in 3-level systems driven by a single pump wave. If there is *no mixing* between the two excited states of the system, quantum interference is found to produce induced transparency on the 12 transition above a threshold corresponding to the optical saturation of the transition. If the two excited states are *mixed or coupled* by a configuration interaction of strength V for example, transparency appears due to Fano resonance on the 13 transition. Interestingly, in each of these cases, gain appears even though the populations of states 1 and 3 always exceed that of state 2, and no special tuning requirement needs to be met [23]. Thus, lasing without inversion takes place at all frequencies close to either ω_{12} or ω_{13} depending on whether there is significant excited state mixing or not. In addition, the 12 transition in particular has gain over a range of red-detuned frequencies near the ω_{12} resonance. Therefore, self-cooled lasing without inversion may be possible.

To examine the behavior of this system, when irradiated by a single pump wave of frequency ω tuned near the 12 transition frequency, the imaginary part of the susceptibility must be calculated. To do this, one can determine the density matrix elements ρ_{ij} between states i and j in the expression [23]

$$\chi''(\omega) = \text{Im}\left\{\left(\frac{2N}{\varepsilon_0 E_0}\right)\left(\mu_{12}\tilde{\rho}_{21} + \mu_{13}\tilde{\rho}_{31}^{(-)} + \mu_{31}\tilde{\rho}_{13}^{(-)} + \mu_{32}\tilde{\rho}_{23}\right)\right\}. \tag{12}$$

Optical absorption is proportional to $\chi''(\omega)$. Hence, when the expression in Equation (12) is evaluated, the absorption and gain spectra can be plotted. When the optical frequency is close to ω_{12} or ω_{13}, the rotating wave approximation (RWA) can be made for the corresponding off-diagonal matrix elements, but not for the 13 transition. This accounts for the co- and counter-rotating terms ($\tilde{\rho}_{31}^{(-)}$ and $\tilde{\rho}_{13}^{(-)}$, respectively) in Equation (12). To plot the response near the 13 transition frequency, the RWA can be applied to the 13 transition but not to the other two. These requirements arise because of the relative placement of the levels assumed in Figure 7, which reflect those of Ce^{3+}. Steady-state expressions for the various matrix elements obtained by third-order perturbation theory are given in Appendix A. The absorption spectra showing the effects of the two types of quantum interference described above are presented in Section 3.

3. Methods and Results

3.1. Improved Cooling via Saturation of Background Absorption in Yb:LiYF$_4$

Laser cooling was investigated in a crystal of 10% Yb^{3+}:YLF, and its efficiency was measured by two different methods, namely Differential Luminescence Thermometry (DLT) and Thermal Lens Spectroscopy (TLS). The Yb^{3+}:YLF sample had dimensions of $3.4 \times 5.1 \times 5.6$ mm^3 and was supported by an aerogel disk (Classic Silica Disk, Aerogel Technologies) to minimize the conductive thermal load. A tunable Ti:Sapphire laser (M Squared SolsTiS) was used as the excitation source. To study the intensity dependence, the pump beam radius at the sample was varied by using different focal length lenses and measuring the spot size with a beam profiler (Thorlabs BC106-VIS). When the pump beam was introduced into the sample, temperature changes and thermal lensing were measured by the DLT and TLS methods, respectively. Cooling efficiency was then computed based on these measurements and found to be intensity-dependent.

3.1.1. Differential Luminescence Thermometry (DLT)

DLT was employed to deduce the crystal temperature from variations of the fluorescence line shape [3]. The infrared fluorescence was collected with a multimode optical fiber (Ocean Optics QP600-2-VIS-NIR; NA = 0.4) connected to a 0.25 m grating spectrometer (Oriel 74100) equipped with a CCD detector (Andor DU491A-1.7). The difference between the measurement and the reference was spectrally integrated to calculate the DLT signals, which were pre-calibrated by the direct heating or cooling of the sample using a temperature controller (Quantum Northwest Flash 300) with an accuracy of ±0.01 K. A thermal camera (FLIR A655sc) was used to monitor the crystal surface temperature and cross-check the temperature measured by DLT [24]. Figures 8 and 9 plot the crystal temperature change versus the time measured by DLT at wavelengths of 1015 nm and 920 nm, showing the representative signals for the cooling and heating ranges.

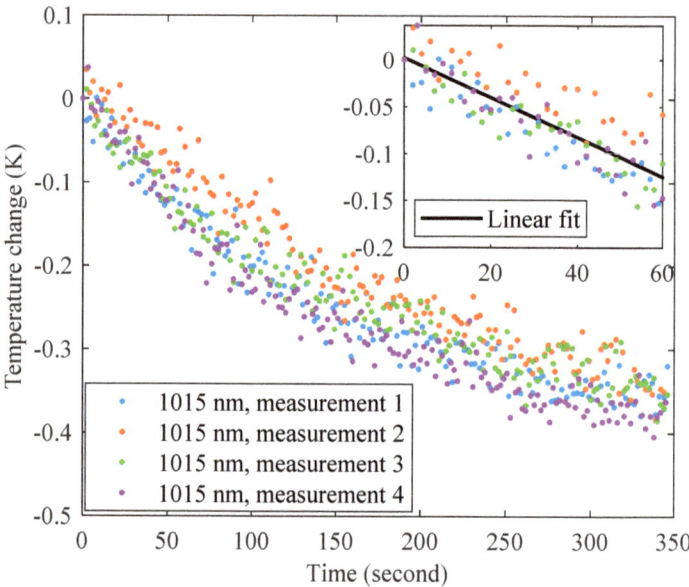

Figure 8. Temperature vs time after the cooling beam is introduced into the Yb:YLF sample. Data were obtained by the DLT method with pump power of 0.8 W at $\lambda = 1015$ nm. At this wavelength, the sample cools. A linear fit to the temperature change during the first minute had a slope of -2.11×10^{-3} K/s (inset).

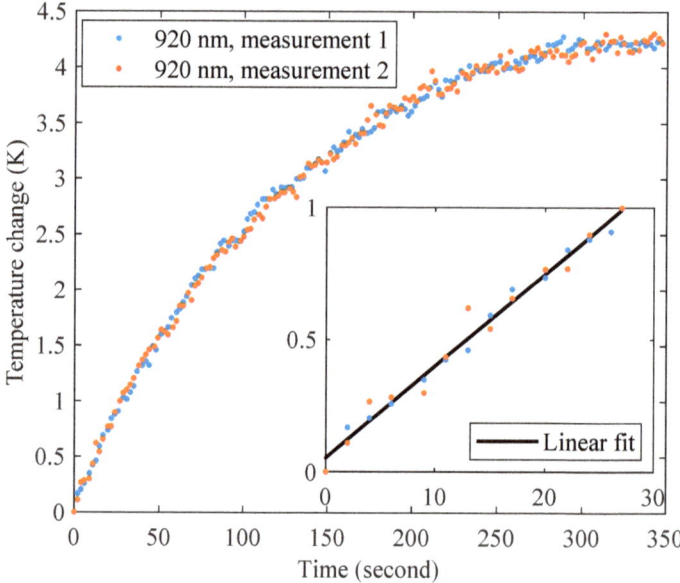

Figure 9. Temperature change versus time based on DLT measurements in Yb:YLF with pump power of 0.8 W at $\lambda = 920$ nm. At this wavelength, the sample heats. A linear fit to the temperature change for the initial excursion in temperature of $\Delta T = 1$ K had a slope of 3.48×10^{-2} K/s (inset).

The cooling efficiency can be computed directly from the temperature evolution measurements. Assuming a crystal of thermal emissivity ε and a surface area A_{surf} enclosed by a blackbody, the thermal balance equation relating the various contributions to heating power at a crystal temperature of T [25,26] is:

$$cM\frac{dT}{dt} = -\eta_c P_{abs} + A_{surf}\varepsilon\sigma_B\left(T_0^4 - T^4\right) + \left(h_c A_{surf} + k\frac{A}{L}\right)(T_0 - T), \quad (13)$$

where σ_B, T_0, h_c, k, A, and L are the Stefan–Boltzmann constant, environmental temperature, convective heat transfer coefficient, thermal conductivity of the link, cross-sectional area, and sample length, respectively. The specific heat c of 10% Yb:YLF is 0.79 J/(g K) at room temperature [27]. The crystal mass ($M = 0.408$ g) was determined using a precision balance (QUINTIX213-1S) with an accuracy of 0.001 g.

The first term on the right side of Equation (13) is the laser-induced heat density. The second term is the power exchange between the crystal and its surroundings through blackbody radiation. The last term is the conductive heat load, which takes into account the contact with the air and sample support. The blackbody radiation and conductive heat load depend on the temperature difference between the crystal and the environment. As indicated by the data of Figures 8 and 9, the temperature change is linear at very short times, reflecting the negligible difference between T and T_0 in the second and third terms on the right of Equation (13). During the first minute after the pump beam enters the sample, only the first term on the right of Equation (13) is responsible for the temperature changes of the crystal. This term is numerically equal to the cooling power; so, the cooling power can be determined directly from the initial slope of the sample temperature versus time. At long times, the difference between T and T_0 increases. Consequently, the last two terms in Equation (13) become significant, and the temperature dependence on time becomes nonlinear. By restricting the data analysis to the early times (or to temperature excursions $dT < 1$ K) and the measuring power absorbed by the sample, the blackbody radiation and conduction terms can be ignored, permitting the cooling efficiency to be determined directly from Equation (13) in a simple way.

When the second and third terms on the right side of Equation (13) can be ignored, the thermal balance equation reduces to $\eta_c = P_{abs}^{-1} cMdT/dt$. The temperature derivative with time can then be determined by applying a linear fit to the data (for temperature changes of less than 1 Kelvin or at times of less than 1 min, whichever occurs first). Examples of such fits are plotted in the insets of Figures 8 and 9. By measuring the injected, reflected, and transmitted pump power, the absorbed power can also be determined. Thus, the cooling efficiency can be measured directly from the temperature evolution measurements.

3.1.2. Thermal Lens Spectroscopy (TLS)

TLS was used to measure the thermal lensing signal by probing the refractive index variation of the crystal induced by a pump beam. The tunable Ti:Sapphire laser was used to pump the crystal and, by chopping its beam, synchronous detection was enabled. In general, two lensing effects are induced by the pump—a fast transient from photoinduced population transfer between the ground and excited states and a slower transient from thermal diffusion. Both of these lensing effects change the refractive index of the crystal and must be accurately modeled to account for their separate contributions [27,28]. The TLS signal was obtained by measuring the intensity variation of a co-propagating He-Ne probe laser (Melles Griot 25-LHP-991-249), which sensed the crystal refractive index changes. Two normalized TLS signals and fits accounting for population and thermal effects [29] are shown in Figure 10. These best fits provided quantitative values for the thermal lens strength and the corresponding cooling efficiency η_c derived from it.

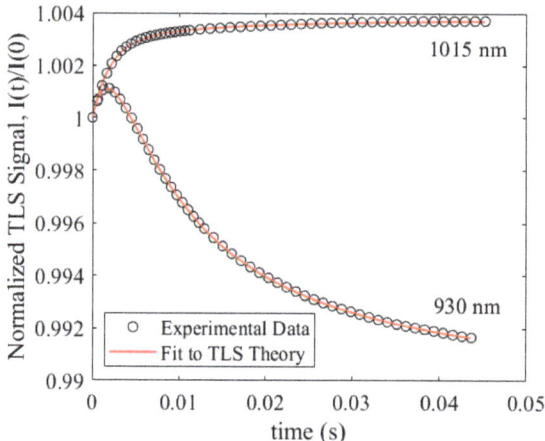

Figure 10. Normalized TLS signal versus time at 1015 nm and 930 nm, showing cooling and heating results in Yb:YLF, respectively. Black circles are the measured TLS signal, and red curves are best fits that account for population and thermal effects.

The cooling efficiency determined at different intensities is plotted versus wavelength in Figures 11 and 12, based on the TLS and DLT data, respectively. The measured pump radii and intensities are shown in Table 1. The main result to note is a steepening of the cooling efficiency curve over most of the range as intensity is increased. This behavior arises from the different variations of the saturation intensity of the coolant and the impurity ions versus the wavelength, as discussed further below and in Ref. [30]. This effect, referred to here as differential absorption saturation, was observed in both the DLT and the TLS experiments and can be explained using the analysis of Section 2.1.

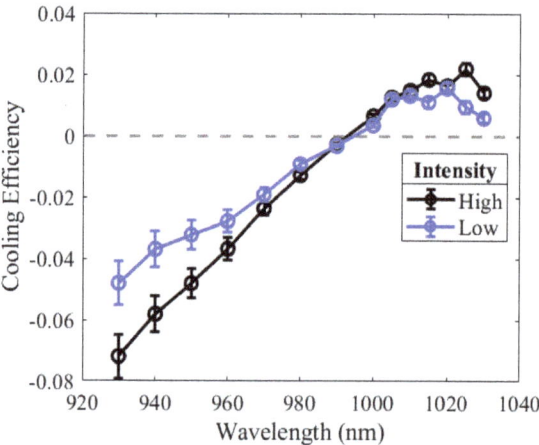

Figure 11. Experimentally determined cooling efficiencies versus wavelength from TLS measurements in Yb:YLF at high and low intensities. Input powers in the range 50–530 mW focused to the tabulated spot sizes, and the resulting intensities are listed in Table 1. A host parameter value of $\Theta = 1.4$ W^{-1} was used for analysis at all intensities. For low and high intensity data, the external quantum efficiency and the background absorption coefficient determined from fitting the data to Equation (10) were $\eta_{ext} = 1.01 \pm 0.02$ and $\alpha_b = (4 \pm 2) \times 10^{-3}$ cm^{-1}.

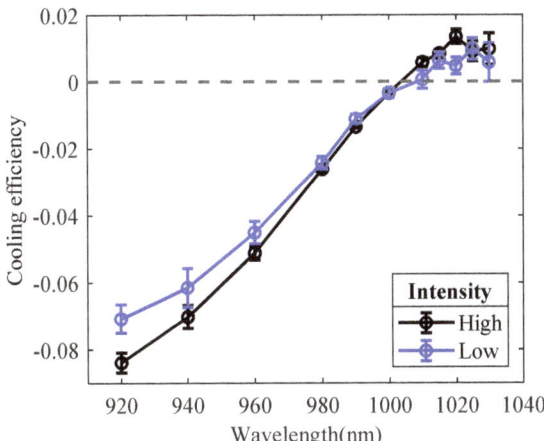

Figure 12. Experimentally determined cooling efficiencies versus wavelength from DLT measurements in Yb:YLF at high and low intensities. The pump power was 0.8 W for all the measurements, and beam size was varied to reach the intensities shown in Table 1.

Table 1. Pump beam radius (half-width at $1/e^2$ intensity) and intensity values used for the measurements presented in Figures 11 and 12. Entries indicate the small variations of intensity at multiple wavelengths for each intensity category.

	Beam Radius (μm)	Intensity (W/cm^2)
DLT High	32.4–39.3	(1.6–2.4) × 10^4
DLT Low	284–318	(2.0–3.3) × 10^2
TLS High	316–364	(1.1–1.3) × 10^3
TLS Low	316–364	(1.1–1.3) × 10^2

The experimental cooling efficiency data coalesce at 1000 nm. There, all the curves pass through the same point, as predicted by the theory of Section 2. At such a crossing point, the cooling efficiency is clearly independent of intensity, indicating the saturation intensity of the background equals the saturation intensity of the coolant ions, which is $\sim 2.6 \times 10^4$ W/cm^2. At longer wavelengths in the cooling range, a significantly higher cooling efficiency is observed at high pump intensity in both sets of data. The results are therefore consistent with a saturation intensity for background impurities that is less than that of the coolant ions, leading to reduced parasitic heating and higher cooling efficiency. At wavelengths shorter than 1000 nm, closer to the main absorption peak of Yb^{3+}, the cooling efficiency drops at high intensity, consistent with a drop in the Yb^{3+} saturation intensity as resonance is approached. The separation of the experimental curves is somewhat larger than the theoretical efficiency curves of Figure 3. In the short wavelength range, this may be attributable to the easy saturation of Yb^{3+}, which would maintain the maximum population density in the excited state, thereby enhancing the well-known energy transfer from Ytterbium to other rare-earth ions such as Erbium [31,32]. The characteristic green upconversion emission of Erbium was in fact visible to the eye. Enhanced energy transfer to the Erbium present as an unintended impurity would elevate the heating load, leading to a lower cooling efficiency at high intensity.

3.2. Laser Cooling on an Electric-Dipole-Allowed Transition in Ti:Al$_2$O$_3$

A Ti^{3+}:Al$_2$O$_3$ sample (GT Advanced Technologies) was grown using the heat exchange method (HEM) known to produce high-quality crystals with exceptionally high figures of merit. In this material, the figure of merit (FOM) is defined as the ratio of the absorption coefficients at two specific wavelengths ($\alpha_{532nm}/\alpha_{800nm}$) and is used as a measure of crystal quality and laser performance. The GTAT sample had a quoted FOM of 844 and was Brewster-cut with the dimensions of 4 × 5 × 20 mm³. The normalized absorption and emission spectra of this sample are shown in Figure 13. Two other laser-grade samples with lower FOMs were included in the cooling tests.

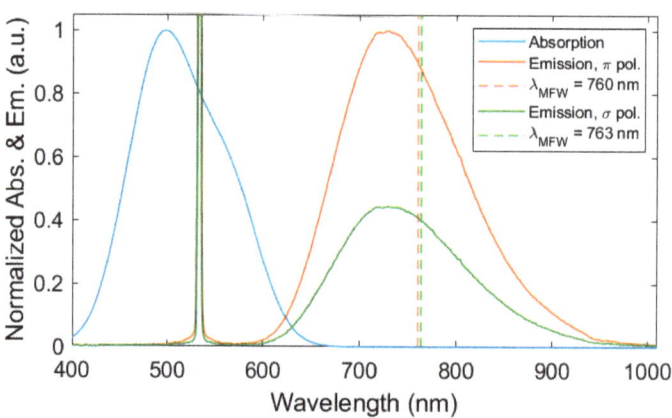

Figure 13. Normalized absorption (blue), π-polarized emission (orange), and σ-polarized emission (green) spectra of Ti^{3+}:Al$_2$O$_3$ (GTAT sample). Dashed vertical lines indicate the calculated mean fluorescent wavelengths (MFW) for emission spectra.

Thermal lens spectroscopy (TLS) in a mode-mismatched configuration [28] was used to investigate the thermal characteristics of the three sapphire samples for pump light tuned close to the absorption peak of Ti^{3+} and in the absorption tail. An experimental approach that corrects for intensity variations of the pump laser [33] was applied in experiments on Yb:YLF but not in the GTAT sapphire sample because weak fluorescence prevented any reliable correction. A weak helium-neon laser ($\lambda_p = 633$ nm) was used as the probe laser. A test was performed with a thermal camera to ensure that the probe power was low enough to avoid any detectable heating. The GTAT sample was first pumped with 532 nm light (Coherent Verdi V6) to show heating. The TLS transient signal for this excitation wavelength (Figure 14a) shows the positive slope expected for a material with $ds/dT > 0$ with increasing temperature. To pump at red-detuned wavelengths in the absorption tail, the tunable Ti:Sapphire laser was used. For some wavelengths longer than the mean fluorescence wavelength, the slope of the TLS signal then became negative, as shown in Figure 14b, which was indicative of sample cooling within the pumping region. Using the known material parameters and the measured experimental values, in both cases, the data fit very well with TLS theory. The TLS signals in the other samples showed only positive sloping curves, such as that in Figure 14a, at all wavelengths.

Interestingly, the cooling behavior at wavelengths longer than the mean fluorescence wavelength was not uniform. Instead, sharp resonances were observed at which heating abruptly switched to cooling. This behavior is shown as TLS signals with negative polarity at discrete wavelengths in Figure 15, consistent with the discussion of Section 2.2 and Figure 5. In the case of well-defined local or host optical phonons, the cooling transitions should be discrete. The spectrum of infrared-active modes is well-known for sapphire [21], but the frequencies of local modes exhibiting site-dependent perturbations with respect to host modes are not. Nevertheless, the cooling resonances observed in Figure 15a,b are well accounted for by assignments that assume four mildly perturbed sites for Ti^{3+} ions in sapphire, as listed in Tables 2 and 3.

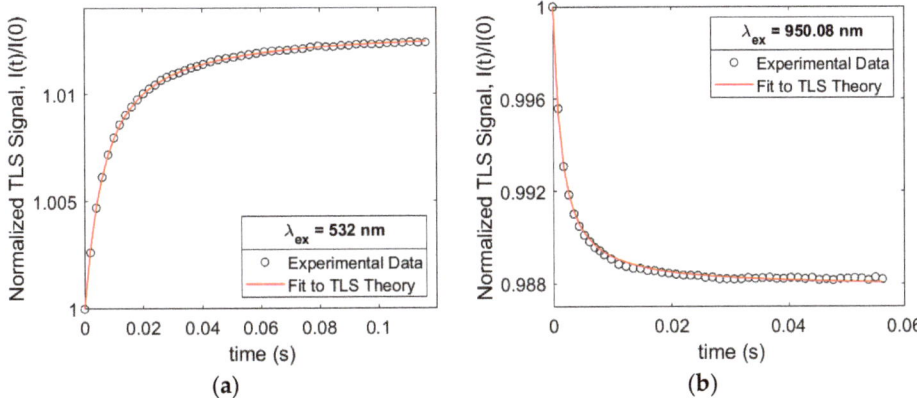

Figure 14. TLS transient signals for excitation wavelengths in the (**a**) absorptive (heating) and (**b**) emissive (cooling) spectral ranges in 0.02% $Ti^{3+}:Al_2O_3$. Black circles are the measured TLS signal, and red curves are best fits that account for only thermal effects.

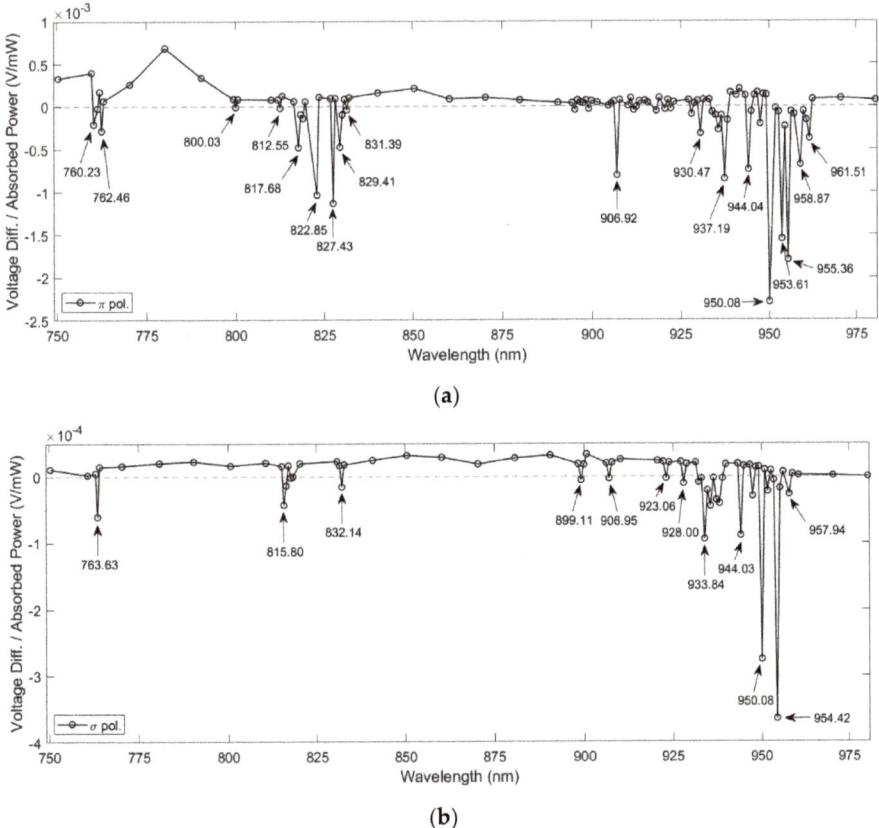

Figure 15. TLS signal versus wavelength in $Ti:Al_2O_3$ for (**a**) π-polarization and (**b**) σ-polarization. Positive signals correspond to heating; negative signals correspond to net cooling of the sample. Wavelength tuning was not continuous but proceeded in ~0.3 nm steps.

Table 2. Assignments of cooling resonances in Ti:Al$_2$O$_3$ for π-polarization (mean fluorescence wavelength 760 nm). Wavenumbers for observed and calculated resonances are subtracted for comparison in the last column on the right. The average discrepancy is given in the bottom row.

λ_{obs} (nm)	k_{obs} (cm^{-1})	Initial Level	Site	k_{calc} (cm^{-1})	$k_{obs} - k_{calc}$ (cm^{-1})
812.55	12,306.93	(^{2}A(0), v$_d$)	3	12,276.79	−30.14
817.68	12,229.72	(^{2}A(0), v$_d$)	4	12,276.79	47.07
822.85	12,152.88	(^{2}A(1), v = 0)	1	11,957.89	−194.99
827.43	12,085.61	(^{2}A(1), v = 0)	2	11,957.89	−127.72
829.41	12,056.76	(^{2}A(1), v = 0)	3	11,957.89	−98.87
831.39	12,028.05	(^{2}A(1), v = 0)	4	11,957.89	−70.15
906.92	11,026.33	(^{2}A(1), v$_d$)	2	11,076.89	50.56
930.47	10,747.26	(^{2}A(1), v$_d$)	3	11,076.89	329.64
937.19	10,670.19	(^{2}A(1), v$_d$)	4	11,076.89	406.70
944.04	10,592.77	(^{2}A(2), v = 0)	1	10,547.89	−44.88
950.08	10,525.43	(^{2}A(2), v = 0)	2	10,547.89	22.47
953.61	10,486.47	(^{2}A(2), v = 0)	3	10,547.89	61.43
955.36	10,467.26	(^{2}A(2), v = 0)	4	10,547.89	80.64
958.87	10,428.94	(^{2}A(2), v$_a$)	1	10,149.89	−279.05
961.51	10,400.31	(^{2}A(2), v$_a$)	2	10,149.89	−250.41
				Average:	−1.21

Table 3. Assignments of cooling resonances in Ti:Al$_2$O$_3$ for σ-polarization (mean fluorescence wavelength 763 nm). Wavenumbers for observed and calculated resonances are subtracted for comparison in the last column on the right. The average discrepancy is given in the bottom row.

λ_{obs} (nm)	k_{obs} (cm^{-1})	Initial Level	Site	k_{calc} (cm^{-1})	$k_{obs} - k_{calc}$ (cm^{-1})
815.80	12,257.91	(^{2}A(0), v$_d$)	4	12,199.56	−58.35
832.14	12,017.21	(^{2}A(1), v = 0)	4	11,906.16	−111.05
899.11	11,122.11	(^{2}A(1), v$_d$)	1	10,999.56	−122.55
906.95	11,025.97	(^{2}A(1), v$_d$)	2	10,999.56	−26.41
928.00	10,775.86	(^{2}A(1), v$_d$)	3	10,999.56	223.70
933.84	10,708.47	(^{2}A(1), v$_d$)	4	10,999.56	291.09
944.03	10,592.88	(^{2}A(2), v = 0)	1	10,496.16	−96.72
950.08	10,525.43	(^{2}A(2), v = 0)	2	10,496.16	−29.27
954.42	10,477.57	(^{2}A(2), v = 0)	3	10,496.16	18.59
957.90	10,439.50	(^{2}A(2), v = 0)	4	10,496.16	56.66
				Average:	13.24

Although the observed resonances were grouped into sets of four perturbed site transitions for the purpose of making transition assignments, the tabulations were based purely on unperturbed host vibrational modes and electronic splitting of the ground state. Absorption transitions at wavelengths on the low energy side of the mean fluorescence wavelength 760 nm were calculated by subtracting the vibrational mode frequencies [21] or electronic splitting [22] (in cm^{-1}) for the listed transitions from the mean fluorescence wavenumber 13,158 cm^{-1} (π-polarization only). The mean fluorescence wavelength for σ-polarization was 763 nm. Despite the lack of information from the literature on site perturbations, agreement between the observed and the calculated resonant wavelengths in the tables was found to be remarkably good. The width of the resonances was close to the step-size tuning of the laser, consistent with the low damping parameters of the optical modes in sapphire [21]. The number of observed cooling resonances in the range of 750–790 nm also decreased when the optical polarization was rotated from π to σ, consistent with higher losses from the impurity background absorption for σ-polarization [34]. This quenching of resonances in σ-polarization was therefore ascribed to increased background heating over much of the spectral range.

3.3. Fano Resonance and Induced Transparency in Laser Cooling

The 3-level system of Ce^{3+} can be viewed either as a Λ-system or a V-system with a large detuning from at least one of the three transitions. The validity of these two perspectives explains why two forms of quantum interference are possible in this system, namely Fano resonance [35] and induced transparency [36,37]. The former requires mixing of the two distinct excited states by some interaction (V-picture), and the latter does not (Λ-picture). The two features that result from interference are the negative peaks displayed in the plots of Figure 16a,b respectively, which display results calculated from Equation (12) using input parameters [38] that specialize the problem to Ce^{3+}: $LiCaAlF_6$.

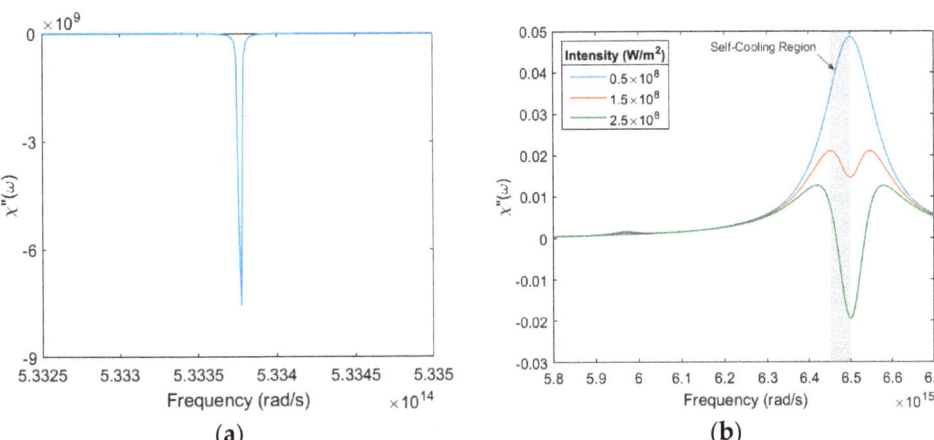

Figure 16. Plots of optical absorption versus frequency in a 3-level system modeled after Ce^{3+}:$LiCaAlF_6$ showing (**a**) a gain feature on the low frequency transition at ω_{13} for an intensity of $I = 0.5 \times 10^8$ W/m^2 and coupling parameter $V/\hbar = 10^8$ rad/s and (**b**) the two short wavelength transitions of Ce^{3+} at low-, medium-, and high-intensity, with $V = 0$. Negative absorption indicates gain without population inversion as the populations of states 1 and 3 exceed that of state 2 at all intensities. The shaded spectral region at red detunings within a linewidth of the ω_{12} transition illustrates the range over which self-cooled LWI may be possible.

In Figure 16a, the coupling frequency was assumed to have a value of $V/\hbar = 10^8$ rad/s. This is considerably less than known optical dephasing and decay parameters of trivalent Ce ions in $LiCaAlF_6$ [37]: $\Gamma_{12} = 10^{12}$ rad/s, $\Gamma_{23} = 10^{12}$ rad/s, $\gamma_{12} = 3.3 \times 10^7$ s^{-1}, $\gamma_{13} = 1.0 \times 10^4$ s^{-1}, and $\gamma_{23} = 1.1 \times 10^7$ s^{-1}. In Figure 16b, its value was set to $V/\hbar = 0$ rad/s. The negative absorption (gain) peak in Figure 16a disappeared when the coupling frequency was set equal to zero. In addition, this feature was found to appear at arbitrary intensity of the pump wave. This identifies it as a Fano resonance that results in gain when the system is pumped at frequency ω_{13}. At the low pump intensity assumed in the plot ($I \sim 10^8$ W/m^2) it may also readily be confirmed that the upper state 3 of the transition is less populated than the ground state 1, showing that lasing without inversion can take place under these circumstances. For example, the steady-state solution for the ratio of populations in states 2 and 3 is $\rho_{22}/\rho_{33} = \gamma_{13}/\gamma_{12}$, which is always small when state 3 is metastable. Near the ω_{12} resonance in Figure 16b, negative absorption (gain) is also induced, but only above a threshold value of pump intensity. The apparent need to meet a threshold requirement for the appearance of gain, in this case, indicates an induced transparency origin of the interference.

Figure 17 presents the theoretical cooling efficiency of Ce^{3+} ions in the wavelength range where the absorption and emission curves overlap. Net cooling is possible from 293–310 nm on the red side of the ω_{12} resonance when the quantum efficiency is one. This range encroaches on the shaded region of Figure 16b, where lasing without inversion can take place. Hence, self-cooled lasing without inversion may be possible in this system. While no experiments have been performed to date to test this prediction, this intriguing possibility indicates that quantum interference could play a role in future schemes for the laser cooling of solids.

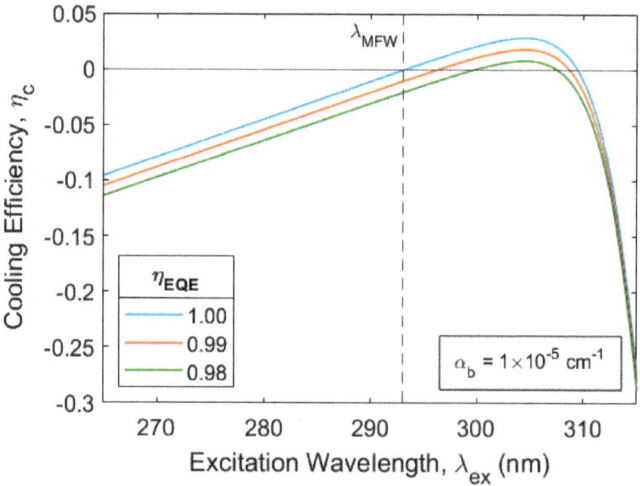

Figure 17. Plot of theoretical cooling efficiency versus pump wavelength of Ce^{3+} ions in $LiCaAlF_6$ obtained from Equation (10) Cooling curves are shown for three different values of external quantum efficiency, assuming a background impurity absorption coefficient of $\alpha_b = 1 \times 10^{-5}$ cm^{-1}. Peak cooling efficiency occurs at 305 nm but extends from 293–310 nm for unity quantum efficiency.

4. Discussion

Laser cooling efficiencies in 10% Yb:YLF, measured with the DLT and TLS methods at various intensities and wavelengths, were in satisfactory mutual agreement. Absorption saturation of the background impurity was observed at high pump intensity, leading to a significantly higher cooling efficiency, as predicted by the differential absorption saturation theory. A method for measuring the saturation intensity of background impurities was devised based on identifying the cross-over point in the intensity-dependent cooling efficiency plot. Our experiments were in close agreement with analysis incorporating saturation effects, revealing that because background absorption can be reduced at high pump intensity, higher pump power reduced parasitic heating and enhanced cooling efficiency. This finding may allow the attainment of lower minimum temperatures and will promote the use of cooling materials that are not well developed and suffer from higher background impurity levels, such as KYW [24]. In addition, this result should enable laser refrigeration of some impure materials that could not be cooled previously at all.

The method used to determine the saturation intensity of background absorption consisted of systematic measurements of laser cooling efficiency by Differential Luminescence Thermometry (DLT) and Thermal Lens Spectroscopy (TLS) versus wavelength and incident intensity. The slope of cooling efficiency versus wavelength exhibited an intensity dependence with a common intersection point at $\lambda = 1000$ nm in the 10% Yb^{3+}:YLF sample, indicating that at this wavelength, the saturation intensities of the coolant ions and background impurities had the same value ($\sim 2.6 \times 10^4$ W/cm^2). For wavelengths longer than 1000 nm, higher pump intensities improved the cooling efficiency significantly, agreeing well with the differential saturation model using the measured saturation intensities.

Although major efforts have been made to improve crystal purity in hosts such as YLF to reach low temperatures by conventional ASF, the present results on improved cooling efficiency through optical saturation establish a new route for lowering the minimum achievable temperatures below those previously possible at a given background absorption level. However, it should be noted that room temperature measurements are insufficient to predict outcomes at cryogenic temperatures. The absorption coefficients of coolant ions and background impurities decrease with temperature [39], resulting in temperature-dependent saturation intensities. It is only in the case when the background absorption saturates first, at an intensity lower than the coolant ions, that lower minimum temperatures can be realized by increasing pump intensity.

The intensity dependence of the cooling efficiency observed in this work is surprising because the saturation intensity of the background impurity absorption is unexpectedly low. This result must stem from a dominant impurity of particular valence and site symmetry. Iron is thought to be the main source of background absorption in Yb:YLF crystals [40]. This impurity is likely a substituent at the trivalent sites (Y^{3+}) in YLF, which would render it predominantly trivalent. It is therefore of possible interest to note that trivalent iron in a material such as Fe:YAG has a low-energy excited state transition from $^6A_{1g}$ to $^4T_{1g}$, which is forbidden by both spin and parity selection rules [41]. Associated with the forbidden transition is a long-lived excited state with a fluorescence lifetime of 170 μs [42], making the transition easy to saturate. The resonance wavelength of this forbidden transition is 903 nm in YAG, with an absorption cross-section of ~1.2×10^{-20} cm^2 at 1000 nm [19]. Unfortunately, the emission cross-section in YAG and both the absorption and emission cross-sections in $LiYF_4$ are currently unknown. However, based on the spectroscopy of Fe:YAG, it is reasonable to surmise that the background saturation intensity of trivalent iron in $LiYF_4$ could be extremely low in the same wavelength range. Using solely the value of the cross-section given above, the absorption saturation intensity of Fe^{3+} is estimated to be 20% lower than that of Yb^{3+} at 1000 nm, which is in quite good agreement with the experimental background saturation intensity reported here (albeit in a different material). For iron in other valence states, such as Fe^{2+} or Fe^{4+} ions, the transition near 1000 nm is allowed [43]. This would lead to a short-lived excited state and a much higher saturation intensity compared with Fe^{3+}. Thus, the divalent and tetravalent ions would not be expected to saturate at the low intensity measured in our experiments. However, these valence states may be less prevalent in YLF than the trivalent state. Hence, one could reasonably conclude that iron impurities may saturate easily and that the cooling efficiency should improve substantially if a sizeable fraction of background impurities become non-absorbing. The properties of trivalent iron seem consistent with the low-absorption saturation intensity determined in our experiments.

Of course, a low value of background saturation intensity could arise from impurities other than iron. Several elements are significantly correlated with the background absorption in crystalline Yb:YLF [40], such as vanadium and chromium. Some of these elements could also lead to a low ionic saturation intensity near 1000 nm. For example, when the transition metal chromium is in the quadrivalent state in a YAG host, the saturation intensity of Cr^{4+} is estimated to be only 10% of Yb^{3+} at 1000 nm [44]. Consequently, the absorption of a variety of background ionic species could saturate similarly at relatively low intensities, contributing to the overall reduction in parasitic heating and enhanced cooling at elevated pump powers. Although we cannot state for certain what impurities contribute to heightened efficiency with increasing pump intensity in Yb:YLF, it seems evident that the dominant transition metal ion and others present in this crystal have properties that are consistent with the low saturation intensity we determined at $\lambda_{cr} = 1000$ nm.

Our TLS experiments also indicate that laser cooling can take place on dipole-allowed transitions. The curves in Figures 10 and 14, which show heating and cooling at wavelengths shorter and longer than the mean fluorescence wavelengths of the corresponding ions, respectively, are qualitatively the same for Yb^{3+}:$LiYF_4$ (dipole-forbidden) and Ti^{3+}:Al_2O_3 (dipole-allowed). The cooling behavior observed in Ti^{3+}:Al_2O_3 reveals that configuration relaxation can be avoided by tuning to wavelengths longer than the mean fluorescence wavelength. This wavelength condition also determines the cooling range of rare-earth ions such as Yb^{3+}. However, the allowed transition of Ti^{3+} has a much faster decay rate; so, faster cool-down times could be enabled for semiconductor sensor circuitry grown on $Ti^{3+}:Al_2O_3$ substrates and cooled optically to cryogenic temperatures. Sapphire is an excellent substrate for GaN, $Al_xGa_{1-x}N$ or $In_xGa_{1-x}N$, and ZnO epitaxy [21,45,46]; so, if cooling were to be demonstrated with laser diodes, the improved performance of imaging arrays in outer space could be achieved in the near future.

In view of the general agreement between calculated and observed wavelengths in Tables 2 and 3, it can be concluded that the discrete resonances in cooling response in $Ti:Al_2O_3$ (Figure 15) arise from absorptions on all-electronic transitions or optical phonon sidebands. The discrepancies between the calculated and observed wavenumbers were less than $\sim$400 cm^{-1} in all cases (<3%) and better than 1.2 cm^{-1} (<0.01%) on average for fifteen π resonances and 60 cm^{-1} (<5.6%) on average for ten σ resonances. Experimentally, more resonances were observed for π- than σ-polarization, even though σ-polarization excites more optical modes in sapphire [21]. Whether or not a particular absorption transition gives rise to observable cooling in $Ti^{3+}:Al_2O_3$ seems to be dictated by the level of background impurity absorption. The background absorption coefficient for σ-polarization has a peak in the 750–790 nm range, with a value nearly twice that for π-polarization [34]. So, more resonances may be observed in this range for π- than for σ-polarization despite the greater number of infrared active E_u modes [21]. The relative efficiencies of cooling transitions also depend on the occupation of the various levels in question, determined by the Boltzmann distribution, and the nature of the transitions, which in general is of mixed electronic and vibrational character. Due to these complexities, initial and final states were assigned to each resonance, but no attempt was made to analyze the relative intensities of the cooling resonances.

Because the dipole-allowed transition of Ti^{3+} has proven useful in this work for the laser cooling of sapphire, the analysis of quantum interference in the 3-level system of Ce^{3+}, which has two such transitions, acquires heightened interest. Trivalent Cerium can undergo quantum interference effects of several kinds. This was evident from the calculations in Figure 16a,b, where gain was induced on the two dipole-allowed absorption transitions by a single incident pump wave. Both figures indicate that lasing without inversion can take place on these transitions as the two lower states are always more occupied than the upper level (given that state 3 is long-lived in Ce^{3+}). Gain on the 13 transition in Figure 16a is due to Fano resonance as it has no threshold and requires the mixing of the excited states ($V \neq 0$). Gain on the 12 transition in Figure 16b is induced only at high pump powers and does not require excited state mixing ($V = 0$). Hence, quantum interference that originates in two distinct ways is possible in this system. At the same time, laser cooling can be sustained theoretically on the red side of the transition at ω_{13}. Therefore, the intriguing possibility emerges of accomplishing self-cooled lasing without inversion in materials with allowed transitions such as $Ce^{3+}:LiCaAlF_6$.

5. Conclusions

Steady-state analysis of ASF laser cooling revealed that improved cooling efficiency becomes possible at elevated pump intensities whenever the saturation intensity of the background absorption is less than that of the coolant ions. Experimental results (Figures 11 and 12) showed that this situation obtains at wavelengths longer than 1000 nm in 10% $Yb:LiYF_4$. In this crystal, the saturation intensity of the background absorption was determined experimentally to be $I_b \sim 2.6 \times 10^4$ W/cm^2, a value low enough to be reached with the continuous-wave excitation used in our experiments. Above this intensity, the cooling efficiency doubled at 1035 nm when input power was increased to the maximum available. This affirmed that in some materials, ASF cooling efficiency could improve with higher pump intensity.

Cooling of bulk sapphire doped with Ti^{3+} ions was also demonstrated on the allowed $^2E \rightarrow {}^2T_2$ transition of the dopant. The polarity of the TLS signals reversed when the wavelength of excitation was tuned from near resonance at 532 nm to wavelengths longer than the mean fluorescence value. The use of Brewster-cut sapphire that was highly purified and lightly doped was essential to minimize losses from the crystal coatings and parasitic absorptions from valence-modified titanium pairs or iron impurities [47–49]. Samples with FOM values less than 800 did not show net laser cooling at any wavelength. Hence, although configuration relaxation on allowed transitions normally contributes to strong heating in optical interactions, cooling is achievable in high-quality $Ti^{3+}:Al_2O_3$ at long wavelengths in the absorption tail. Cooling in sapphire occurred at discrete absorption resonances which were assigned to electronic transitions and optical phonon sidebands. This behavior differed from cooling on forbidden transitions in rare-earth systems where continuous tuning is observed due to the continuous density of states spectrum for the acoustic phonons which mediate refrigeration. Overall, the present results provide accelerated cooling to lower minimum temperatures based on electric-dipole-allowed transitions and optical saturation. These findings should enable Raman cooling, self-cooled lasing without inversion, and other advancements of the field.

Author Contributions: Conceptualization, S.C.R.; methodology, L.B.A., L.C. and S.C.R.; investigation, L.B.A. and L.C.; formal analysis, L.B.A., L.C. and S.C.R.; writing, L.B.A., L.C. and S.C.R.; supervision, S.C.R.; funding acquisition, S.C.R. All authors have read and agreed to the published version of the manuscript.

Funding: This research was funded by the Air Force Office of Scientific Research, MURI grant FA9550-16-1-0383.

Data Availability Statement: All data sets obtained in this research are available upon request from lead author L.B.A.

Acknowledgments: The authors wish to thank Junior R. Silva for the loan of a crystal of 10% $Yb:LiYF_4$.

Conflicts of Interest: The authors declare no conflict of interest.

Appendix A

In this Appendix, with reference to the 3-level system of Figure 7 in the text, density matrix theory is applied to calculate the third-order susceptibility of Ce^{3+} at the pump frequency ω. Two limits are considered to simplify the calculation by choosing frequencies with small detunings from the transition at ω_{12} or the transition at ω_{13}, respectively. This permits the rotating wave approximation (RWA) to be made for off-diagonal matrix elements corresponding to transitions at small detunings from the optical frequency. Transitions with large detunings must retain non-rotating wave terms, which make the calculation more cumbersome.

Explicit results are presented only for the case of optical frequencies close to ω_{12}. In this limit, the RWA is appropriate for the 12 and 23 transitions but not the 13 transition. Hence, the interaction Hamiltonian has the form

$$\begin{aligned} V &= \left\{ \left(\tilde{V}_{12}^{(1)} e^{i\omega t} + \tilde{V}_{32}^{(1)} e^{i\omega t} + \tilde{V}_{13}^{(1+)} e^{i\omega t} + \tilde{V}_{13}^{(1-)} e^{-i\omega t} \right) + c.c. \right\} + \tilde{V}_{32}^{(0)} \\ &= \left\{ \left(-\frac{\hbar\Omega_{12}}{2} e^{i\omega t} - \frac{\hbar\Omega_{32}}{2} e^{i\omega t} - \frac{\hbar\Omega_{13}}{2} e^{i\omega t} - \frac{\hbar\Omega_{13}}{2} \right) + c.c. \right\} + \tilde{V}_{32}^{(0)}, \end{aligned} \tag{A1}$$

where $\tilde{V}_{32}^{(0)}$ is a static mixing interaction of states 2 and 3, and the Rabi frequencies of the optical interaction terms between states i and j are defined by $\Omega_{ij} \equiv \mu_{ij} E_0 / \hbar$. The equation of motion for the density matrix is

$$i\hbar\dot{\rho} = [(H_0 + V), \rho]. \tag{A2}$$

Because the 13 transition is forbidden, the dipole moment is negligible compared to moments on the allowed interactions with small detunings. Hence, we set $V_{13} \approx 0$ and have the following equations for individual matrix elements:

$$i\hbar\dot{\rho}_{11} = (V_{12}\rho_{21} - \rho_{12}V_{21}) + i\hbar\gamma_{21}\rho_{22} + i\hbar\gamma_{31}\rho_{33} \tag{A3}$$

$$i\hbar\dot{\rho}_{22} = -(V_{12}\rho_{21} - \rho_{12}V_{21}) - (V_{32}\rho_{23} - \rho_{32}V_{23}) - i\hbar\gamma_{21}\rho_{22} - i\hbar\gamma_{23}\rho_{22} \tag{A4}$$

$$i\hbar\dot{\rho}_{33} = (V_{32}\rho_{23} - \rho_{32}V_{23}) + i\hbar\gamma_{23}\rho_{22} - i\hbar\gamma_{31}\rho_{33} \tag{A5}$$

$$\dot{\rho}_{12} = i\omega_{12}\rho_{12} + \frac{1}{i\hbar}V_{12}(\rho_{22} - \rho_{11}) - \frac{1}{i\hbar}\rho_{13}V_{32} - \Gamma_{21}\rho_{12} \tag{A6}$$

$$\dot{\rho}_{13} = i\omega_{13}\rho_{13} + \frac{1}{i\hbar}(V_{12}\rho_{23} - \rho_{12}V_{23}) - \Gamma_{31}\rho_{13} \tag{A7}$$

$$\dot{\rho}_{23} = -i\omega_{32}\rho_{23} + \frac{1}{i\hbar}V_{23}(\rho_{33} - \rho_{22}) + \frac{1}{i\hbar}V_{21}\rho_{13} - \Gamma_{32}\rho_{23} \tag{A8}$$

$$\rho_{ji} = \rho_{ij}^*. \tag{A9}$$

As the RWA is not valid on the 13 transition in the present case, the off-diagonal term ρ_{31} must include positive and negative frequency terms. Thus, we assume that

$$\rho_{13} = \tilde{\rho}_{13}^{(+)}e^{i\omega t} + \tilde{\rho}_{13}^{(-)}e^{-i\omega t} \quad \rightarrow \quad \dot{\rho}_{13} = i\omega\tilde{\rho}_{13}^{(+)}e^{i\omega t} - i\omega\tilde{\rho}_{13}^{(-)}e^{-i\omega t} \tag{A10}$$

$$\rho_{31} = \tilde{\rho}_{31}^{(+)}e^{i\omega t} + \tilde{\rho}_{31}^{(-)}e^{-i\omega t} \quad \rightarrow \quad \dot{\rho}_{31} = i\omega\tilde{\rho}_{31}^{(+)}e^{i\omega t} - i\omega\tilde{\rho}_{31}^{(-)}e^{-i\omega t}. \tag{A11}$$

The tilde in these expressions indicates a slowly varying amplitude (whose time derivative may be set to zero). The other coherences in the system have simpler forms and obey the RWA. Thus, we can write

$$\rho_{12} = \tilde{\rho}_{12}e^{i\omega t} \quad \rightarrow \quad \dot{\rho}_{12} = i\omega\tilde{\rho}_{12}e^{i\omega t} \tag{A12}$$

$$\rho_{32} = \tilde{\rho}_{32}e^{i\omega t} \quad \rightarrow \quad \dot{\rho}_{32} = i\omega\tilde{\rho}_{32}e^{i\omega t}. \tag{A13}$$

Using standard perturbation theory [16], the following results are found for the first-order density matrix elements:

$$\tilde{\rho}_{12}^{(1)} = \frac{(\Omega_{12}/2)(\Delta_{13} + i\Gamma_{31}) - \left(V_{32}^{(0)}/\hbar\right)(\Omega_{13}/2)}{(\Delta_{12} + i\Gamma_{12})(\Delta_{13} + i\Gamma_{31}) - \left|\left(V_{23}^{(0)}/\hbar\right)\right|^2} \tag{A14}$$

$$\tilde{\rho}_{13}^{(1+)} = \frac{(\Omega_{13}/2)(\Delta_{12} + i\Gamma_{21}) - (\Omega_{12}/2)\left(V_{23}^{(0)}/\hbar\right)}{(\Delta_{12} + i\Gamma_{21})(\Delta_{13} + i\Gamma_{31}) - \left|\left(V_{23}^{(0)}/\hbar\right)\right|^2} \tag{A15}$$

$$\tilde{\rho}_{31}^{(1-)} = \left[\tilde{\rho}_{13}^{(1+)}\right]^* = \frac{(\Omega_{31}/2)(\Delta_{12} - i\Gamma_{21}) - (\Omega_{21}/2)\left(V_{32}^{(0)}/\hbar\right)}{(\Delta_{12} - i\Gamma_{21})(\Delta_{13} - i\Gamma_{31}) - \left|\left(V_{23}^{(0)}/\hbar\right)\right|^2} \tag{A16}$$

$$\tilde{\rho}_{13}^{(1-)} = \frac{(\Omega_{13}/2)(\Delta_{12} + i\Gamma_{21}) - (\Omega_{12}/2)\left(V_{23}^{(0)}/\hbar\right)}{(\Delta_{12} + i\Gamma_{21})([\omega_{13} + \omega] + i\Gamma_{31}) - \left|\left(V_{23}^{(0)}/\hbar\right)\right|^2} \tag{A17}$$

$$\tilde{\rho}_{31}^{(1+)} = \left[\tilde{\rho}_{13}^{(1-)}\right]^* = \frac{(\Omega_{31}/2)(\Delta_{12} - i\Gamma_{21}) - (\Omega_{21}/2)\left(V_{32}^{(0)}/\hbar\right)}{(\Delta_{12} - i\Gamma_{21})([\omega_{13} + \omega] - i\Gamma_{31}) - \left|\left(V_{23}^{(0)}/\hbar\right)\right|^2} \tag{A18}$$

$$\tilde{\rho}_{32}^{(1)} = \tilde{\rho}_{23}^{(1)*} = 0. \tag{A19}$$

All coherences are zero in the second-order. The results for populations however are

$$\rho_{11}^{(2)} = -\rho_{22}^{(2)} - \rho_{33}^{(2)} \tag{A20}$$

$$\rho_{22}^{(2)} = \frac{1}{\gamma_2} \left\{ \frac{-i|\Omega_{21}/2|^2}{(\Delta_{12} - i\Gamma_{21})} + \frac{i(\Omega_{12}/2)\left(V_{23}^{(0)}/\hbar\right)}{(\Delta_{12} - i\Gamma_{21})} \left\{ \frac{(\Omega_{31}/2)(\Delta_{12} - i\Gamma_{12}) - (\Omega_{21}/2)\left(V_{32}^{(0)}/\hbar\right)}{(\Delta_{12} - i\Gamma_{12})(\Delta_{13} - i\Gamma_{31}) - \left|\left(V_{23}^{(0)}/\hbar\right)\right|^2} \right\} + \cdots \right.$$

$$\left. \cdots + \frac{i|\Omega_{12}/2|^2}{(\Delta_{12} + i\Gamma_{21})} - \frac{i(\Omega_{21}/2)\left(V_{32}^{(0)}/\hbar\right)}{(\Delta_{12} + i\Gamma_{21})} \left\{ \frac{(\Omega_{13}/2)(\Delta_{12} + i\Gamma_{12}) - (\Omega_{12}/2)\left(V_{23}^{(0)}/\hbar\right)}{(\Delta_{12} + i\Gamma_{12})(\Delta_{13} + i\Gamma_{31}) - \left|\left(V_{23}^{(0)}/\hbar\right)\right|^2} \right\} \right\} \quad \text{(A21)}$$

$$\rho_{33}^{(2)} = \frac{1}{\gamma_{31}} \left\{ \frac{1}{i\hbar}\left(V_{31}^{(1+)}\rho_{13}^{(1-)} - \rho_{31}^{(1-)}V_{13}^{(1+)}\right) + \frac{1}{i\hbar}\left(V_{31}^{(1-)}\rho_{13}^{(1+)} - \rho_{31}^{(1+)}V_{13}^{(1-)}\right) + \gamma_{23}\rho_{22}^{(2)} \right\}. \quad \text{(A22)}$$

Finally, in third-order, only the coherences are needed to find the nonlinear polarization of the medium. These off-diagonal elements are

$$\tilde{\rho}_{12}^{(3)} = \frac{(\Omega_{12}/2)}{(\Delta_{12} + i\Gamma_{21})}\left(\rho_{11}^{(2)} - \rho_{22}^{(2)}\right) - \frac{\left(V_{32}^{(0)}/\hbar\right)}{(\Delta_{12} + i\Gamma_{21})}\tilde{\rho}_{13}^{(3)} \quad \text{(A23)}$$

$$\tilde{\rho}_{13}^{(3+)} = \frac{(\Omega_{13}/2)}{(\Delta_{13} + i\Gamma_{31})}\left(\rho_{11}^{(2)} - \rho_{33}^{(2)}\right) - \frac{\tilde{\rho}_{12}^{(3)}\left(V_{23}^{(0)}/\hbar\right)}{(\Delta_{13} + i\Gamma_{31})} \quad \text{(A24)}$$

$$\tilde{\rho}_{13}^{(3-)} = \frac{(\Omega_{13}^*/2)}{(\omega_{13} + \omega + i\Gamma_{31})}\left(\rho_{11}^{(2)} - \rho_{33}^{(2)}\right) \quad \text{(A25)}$$

$$\tilde{\rho}_{23}^{(3)} = \frac{(\Omega_{32}^*/2)}{(\Delta_{32} - i\Gamma_{32})}\left(\rho_{33}^{(2)} - \rho_{22}^{(2)}\right). \quad \text{(A26)}$$

Taking the contributions from various orders into account, the off-diagonal elements are

$$\tilde{\rho}_{21} = \tilde{\rho}_{21}^{(1)} + \tilde{\rho}_{21}^{(3)} \quad \text{(A27)}$$

$$\tilde{\rho}_{13}^{(+)} = \tilde{\rho}_{13}^{(1+)} + \tilde{\rho}_{13}^{(3+)} \quad \text{(A28)}$$

$$\tilde{\rho}_{13}^{(-)} = \tilde{\rho}_{13}^{(1-)} + \tilde{\rho}_{13}^{(3-)} \quad \text{(A29)}$$

$$\tilde{\rho}_{31}^{(-)} = \tilde{\rho}_{31}^{(1-)} + \tilde{\rho}_{31}^{(3-)} = \left[\tilde{\rho}_{13}^{(+)}\right]^* \quad \text{(A30)}$$

$$\tilde{\rho}_{31}^{(+)} = \tilde{\rho}_{31}^{(1+)} + \tilde{\rho}_{31}^{(3+)} = \left[\tilde{\rho}_{13}^{(-)}\right]^* \quad \text{(A31)}$$

$$\tilde{\rho}_{23} = \tilde{\rho}_{23}^{(3)}. \quad \text{(A32)}$$

These results were used to plot the curves in Figure 16b. To plot Figure 16a, the calculation of this section must be repeated on the assumption that the RWA applies to the ω_{13} transition but not the two allowed transitions at frequencies in the neighborhood of the first system resonance. Input parameters for these calculations were as follows:

$$V = V_{23}^{(0)}/\hbar = 10^8 \text{ rad/s}; \; N = 10 \times 10^{21} \text{ m}^{-3}; \; \gamma_{21} = 3.3 \times 10^7 \text{ s}^{-1}; \; \gamma_{23} = 1.1 \times 10^7 \text{ s}^{-1};$$
$$\gamma_{31} = 10^4 \text{ s}^{-1}; \; |\mu_{23}|^2 = 0.333 \times |\mu_{21}|^2.$$

References

1. Epstein, R.I.; Buchwald, M.I.; Edwards, B.C.; Gosnell, T.R.; Mungan, C.E. Observation of laser-induced fluorescent cooling of a solid. *Nature* **1995**, *377*, 500–503. [CrossRef]
2. Bowman, S.R.; Mungan, C.E. New materials for optical cooling. *Appl. Phys. B* **2000**, *71*, 807–811. [CrossRef]
3. Melgaard, S.D.; Albrecht, A.R.; Hehlen, M.P.; Sheik-Bahae, M. Solid-state optical refrigeration to sub-100 Kelvin regime. *Sci. Rep.* **2016**, *6*, 20380. [CrossRef] [PubMed]
4. Hehlen, M.P.; Meng, J.; Albrecht, A.R.; Lee, E.R.; Gragossian, A.; Love, S.P.; Hamilton, C.E.; Epstein, R.I.; Sheik-Bahae, M. First demonstration of an all-solid-state optical cryocooler. *Light Sci. Appl.* **2018**, *7*, 15. [CrossRef] [PubMed]

5. Bowman, S.R. Lasers without internal heat generation. *IEEE J. Quantum Electron.* **1999**, *35*, 115–122. [CrossRef]
6. Bowman, S.R.; O'Connor, S.P.; Biswal, S.; Condon, N.J.; Rosenberg, A. Minimizing Heat Generation in Solid-State Lasers. *IEEE J. Quantum Electron.* **2010**, *46*, 1076–1085. [CrossRef]
7. Yang, Z.; Meng, J.; Albrecht, A.R.; Sheik-Bahae, M. Radiation-balanced Yb:YAG disk laser. *Opt. Express* **2019**, *27*, 1392–1400. [CrossRef]
8. Hehlen, M.P.; Epstein, R.I.; Inoue, H. Model of laser cooling in the Yb^{3+}-doped fluorozirconate glass ZBLAN. *Phys. Rev. B* **2007**, *75*, 144302. [CrossRef]
9. Feofilov, S.P.; Kulinkin, A.B.; Konyushkin, V.A.; Nakladov, A.N. The role of two-step excitation processes in laser cooling experiments: $CaF_2:Eu^{2+}$. *Opt. Mater.* **2016**, *60*, 240. [CrossRef]
10. Khurgin, J.B. Surface plasmon-assisted laser cooling of solids. *Phys. Rev. Lett.* **2007**, *98*, 177401. [CrossRef]
11. Rivlin, L.A.; Zadernovsky, A.A. Laser cooling of semiconductors. *Opt. Commun.* **1997**, *139*, 219–222. [CrossRef]
12. Rupper, G.; Kwong, N.H.; Binder, R. Optical refrigeration of GaAs: Theoretical study. *Phys. Rev. B* **2007**, *76*, 245203. [CrossRef]
13. Nemova, G.; Kashyap, R. Laser Cooling of Solids. *Rep. Prog. Phys.* **2010**, *73*, 086501. [CrossRef]
14. Mungan, C.E.; Gosnell, T. Laser Cooling of Solids. *Adv. At. Mol. Opt. Phys.* **1999**, *40*, 161–228. [CrossRef]
15. Rand, S.C. Raman Laser Cooling of Solids. *J. Lumin.* **2013**, *133*, 10–14. [CrossRef]
16. Zhang, J.; Zhang, Q.; Wang, X.; Kwek, L.C.; Xiong, Q. Resolved-sideband Raman cooling of an optical phonon in semiconductor materials. *Nat. Photon.* **2016**, *10*, 600–605. [CrossRef]
17. Rand, S.C. *Lectures on Light*, 2nd ed.; Oxford University Press: New York, NY, USA, 2016.
18. McCumber, D.E. Einstein Relations Connecting Broadband Emission and Absorption Spectra. *Phys. Rev.* **1964**, *136*, A954–A957. [CrossRef]
19. Püschel, S.; Kalusniak, S.; Kränkel, C.; Tanaka, H. Temperature-dependent radiative lifetime of Yb:YLF: Refined cross sections and potential for laser cooling. *Opt. Express* **2021**, *29*, 11106–11120. [CrossRef]
20. Scott, G.B.; Lacklison, D.E.; Page, J.L. Absorption spectra of $Y_3Fe_5O_{12}$(YIG) and $Y_3Ga_5O_{12}$: Fe^{3+}. *Phys. Rev. B* **1974**, *10*, 971–986. [CrossRef]
21. Schubert, M.; Tiwald, T.E.; Herzinger, C.M. Infrared dielectric anisotropy and phonon modes of sapphire. *Phys. Rev. B* **2000**, *61*, 8187–8201. [CrossRef]
22. Shirakov, A.; Burshtein, Z.; Shimony, Y.; Frumker, E.; Ishaaya, A.A. Radiative and non-radiative transitions of excited Ti^{3+} cations in sapphire. *Sci. Rep.* **2019**, *9*, 18810. [CrossRef]
23. Scully, M.O.; Zubairy, M.S. *Quantum Optics*; Cambridge University Press: Cambridge, UK, 2012.
24. Cheng, L.; Andre, L.B.; Salkeld, A.J.; Andrade, L.H.C.; Lima, S.M.; Silva, J.R.; Rytz, D.; Rand, S.C. Laser cooling of Yb^{3+}:KYW. *Opt. Express* **2020**, *28*, 2778–2788. [CrossRef]
25. de Lima Filho, E.S.; Nemova, G.; Loranger, S.; Kashyap, R. Laser-induced cooling of a Yb:YAG crystal in air at atmospheric pressure. *Opt. Express* **2013**, *21*, 24711–24720. [CrossRef]
26. Seletskiy, D.V.; Melgaard, S.D.; Lieto, A.D.; Tonelli, M.; Sheik-Bahae, M. Laser cooling of a semiconductor load to 165 K. *Opt. Express* **2010**, *18*, 18061–18066. [CrossRef]
27. Aggarwal, R.L.; Ripin, D.J.; Ochoa, J.R.; Fan, T.Y. Measurement of thermo-optic properties of $Y_3Al_5O_{12}$, $Lu_3Al_5O_{12}$, $YAlO_3$, $LiYF_4$, $LiLuF_4$, BaY_2F_8, $KGd(WO_4)_2$, and $KY(WO_4)_2$ laser crystals in the 80–300 K temperature range. *J. App. Phys.* **2005**, *98*, 103514. [CrossRef]
28. Shen, J.; Lowe, R.D.; Snook, R.D. A model for cw laser induced mode-mismatched dual-beam thermal lens spectrometry. *Chem. Phys.* **1992**, *165*, 385–396. [CrossRef]
29. Silva, J.R.; Malacarne, L.C.; Baesso, M.L.; Lima, S.M.; Andrade, L.H.C.; Jacinto, C.; Hehlen, M.P.; Astrath, N.G.C. Modeling the population lens effect in thermal lens spectrometry. *Opt. Lett.* **2013**, *38*, 422–424. [CrossRef] [PubMed]
30. Cheng, L.; Andre, L.B.; Almeida, G.L.; Andrade, L.H.C.; Lima, S.M.; Silva, J.R.; Catunda, T.; Guyot, Y.; Rand, S.C. Differential Absorption Saturation in Laser Cooled Yb:YLF. *Opt. Mat.*. under review.
31. Lieto, A.D.; Sottile, A.; Volpi, A.; Zhang, Z.; Seletskiy, D.V.; Tonelli, M. Influence of other rare earth ions on the optical refrigeration efficiency in Yb:YLF crystals. *Opt. Express* **2014**, *22*, 28572–28583. [CrossRef]
32. Cittadino, G.; Volpi, A.; Lieto, A.D.; Tonelli, M. Co-doping of $LiYF_4$ crystal: A virtuous effect of cooling efficiency. *J. Phys. D: Appl. Phys.* **2018**, *51*, 145302. [CrossRef]
33. Silva, J.R.; Andrade, L.H.C.; Lima, S.M.; Guyot, Y.; Giannini, N.; Sheik-Bahae, M. External Quantum Efficiency determined by combined thermal lens and photoluminescence spectroscopy techniques: Application to Ce^{3+}:YAG. *Appl. Phys. Lett.* **2020**, *117*, 061107. [CrossRef]
34. Moulton, P. Spectroscopic and laser characteristics of $Ti:Al_2O_3$. *J. Opt. Soc. B* **1986**, *3*, 125–133. [CrossRef]
35. Fano, U. Effects of Configuration Interaction on Intensities and Phase Shifts. *Phys. Rev.* **1961**, *124*, 1866–1878. [CrossRef]
36. Boller, K.J.; İmamoğlu, A.; Harris, S.E. Observation of electromagnetically induced transparency. *Phys. Rev. Lett.* **1991**, *66*, 2593. [CrossRef] [PubMed]
37. Anisimov, P.M.; Dowling, J.P.; Sanders, B.C. Objectively Discerning Autler-Townes Splitting from Electromagnetically Induced Transparency. *Phys. Rev. Lett.* **2011**, *107*, 163604. [CrossRef]
38. Marshall, C.D.; Payne, S.A.; Speth, J.A.; Tassano, J.B.; Krupke, W.F.; Quarles, G.J.; Castillo, V.K.; Chai, B.H.T. Properties of $Ce:LiSrAlF_6$ and $Ce:LiCaAlF_6$ ultraviolet lasers. *SPIE Proc.* **1994**, *2115*, 7. [CrossRef]

9. Volpi, A.; Meng, J.; Gragossian, A.; Albrecht, A.R.; Rostami, S.; Lieto, A.D.; Epstein, R.I.; Tonelli, M.; Hehlen, M.P.; Sheik-Bahae, M. Optical refrigeration: The role of parasitic absorption at cryogenic temperatures. *Opt. Express* **2019**, *27*, 29710–29718. [CrossRef]
10. Melgaard, S.; Seletskiy, D.; Polyak, V.; Asmerom, Y.; Sheik-Bahae, M. Identification of parasitic losses in Yb:YLF and prospects for optical refrigeration down to 80K. *Opt. Express* **2014**, *22*, 7756–7764. [CrossRef]
11. Greene, B.I.; Wolfe, R. Femtosecond relaxation dynamics in magnetic garnets. *J. Opt. Soc. Am. B* **1985**, *2*, 600–605. [CrossRef]
12. Pathak, N.; Gupta, S.K.; Sanyal, K.; Kumar, M.; Kadam, R.M.; Natarajan, V. Photoluminescence and EPR studies on Fe^{3+}-doped $ZnAl_2O_4$: An evidence for local site swapping of Fe^{3+} and formation of inverse and normal phase. *Dalton Trans.* **2014**, *43*, 9313–9323. [CrossRef]
13. Gareyeva, Z.V.; Doroshenko, R.A. Optical absorption of octahedral ions Fe^{2+}, Fe^{4+} and photoinduced effect in YIG single crystals. *J. Magn. Magn. Mater.* **2004**, *268*, 1–7. [CrossRef]
14. Ma, J.; Dong, J.; Ueda, K.I.; Kaminskii, A.A. Optimization of Yb:YAG/Cr^{4+}:YAG composite ceramics passively Q-switched microchip lasers. *Appl. Phys. B* **2011**, *105*, 749–760. [CrossRef]
15. See for example: Ryou, J.H. Gallium nitride (GaN) on sapphire substrates for visible LEDs. In *Nitride Semiconductor Light-Emitting Diodes*; Woodhead Publishing: Cambridge, UK, 2014; pp. 66–98. [CrossRef]
16. See for example: Baxter, J.B.; Aydil, E.S. Epitaxial growth of ZnO nanowires on a- and c-plane sapphire. *J. Cryst. Growth* **2005**, *274*, 407–411. [CrossRef]
17. Townsend, M.G. Visible Charge Transfer Band in Blue Sapphire. *Solid State Comm.* **1968**, *6*, 81–83. [CrossRef]
18. Krebs, J.J.; Maisch, W.G. Exchange Effects in the Optical-Absorption Spectrum of Fe^{3+} in Al_2O_3. *Phys. Rev. B* **1971**, *4*, 757. [CrossRef]
19. Ferguson, J.; Fielding, P.E. The Origins of the Colours of Yellow, Green and Blue Sapphires. *Chem. Phys. Lett.* **1971**, *10*, 262. [CrossRef]

Article

Laser Cooling beyond Rate Equations: Approaches from Quantum Thermodynamics

Conor N. Murphy, Luísa Toledo Tude and Paul R. Eastham *

School of Physics, Trinity College Dublin, DN02 PN40 Dublin, Ireland; murphc92@tcd.ie (C.N.M.); toledotl@tcd.ie (L.T.T.)
* Correspondence: easthamp@tcd.ie

Abstract: Solids can be cooled by driving impurity ions with lasers, allowing them to transfer heat from the lattice phonons to the electromagnetic surroundings. This exemplifies a quantum thermal machine, which uses a quantum system as a working medium to transfer heat between reservoirs. We review the derivation of the Bloch-Redfield equation for a quantum system coupled to a reservoir, and its extension, using counting fields, to calculate heat currents. We use the full form of this equation, which makes only the weak-coupling and Markovian approximations, to calculate the cooling power for a simple model of laser cooling. We compare its predictions with two other time-local master equations: the secular approximation to the full Bloch-Redfield equation, and the Lindblad form expected for phonon transitions in the absence of driving. We conclude that the full Bloch-Redfield equation provides accurate results for the heat current in both the weak- and strong- driving regimes, whereas the other forms have more limited applicability. Our results support the use of Bloch-Redfield equations in quantum thermal machines, despite their potential to give unphysical results.

Keywords: quantum thermodynamics; open quantum systems; laser cooling; Bloch-Redfield theory

1. Introduction

Laser cooling [1–3], in both atomic and solid-state systems, is now a well established technique. In solids, particularly rare-earth-doped glasses, cooling can be achieved by using anti-Stokes fluorescence of the dopants. It provides an example of a quantum thermal machine [4–6], in which is a discrete quantum system—in this case, the energy levels of rare earth ion—is the working medium. This working medium couples to two heat baths and a source of work, namely the phonon and photon reservoirs and the driving laser, allowing it to operate as a refrigerator.

Laser cooling is generally modeled using rate equations for the populations of the levels. This approach can also be used for semiconductors, where the rate equations refer to the populations of the electron and hole bands. However, such approaches cannot capture certain effects which, while not expected to be relevant in systems such as rare earths, are increasingly important in quantum thermodynamics more generally. These include the role of coherences in determining heat flows, which have been argued to offer enhanced performances in various quantum thermal machines [7–11]; the effects of strong driving, which can modify the energy levels through the a.c. Stark effect [12–14], and so impact on the heat flows [11,15]; and the effects of spectral structure in the heat baths. This last can be considered in two regimes: for strongly structured baths one can expect non-Markovian behavior [16–18], whose impact on thermodynamics remains a challenging open topic. However, the spectral structure can be important even where a Markovian description remains appropriate [19]. An important practical target for thermodynamic machines is to maximize their power, and the heat flows to a bath are determined by its spectral density. Thus to achieve maximum power one must consider the spectral structure of baths, if there is any on the energy scales of the working medium. Examples of systems where this occurs include quantum-dot excitons coupled to acoustic phonons [20], colour centres in diamond [21,22], and superconducting circuits [23].

These issues can be treated theoretically by studying models of an open quantum system in which the working medium interacts with its surrounding heat baths. Such models are tractable in the weak-coupling, Markovian regime, where they lead to time-local equations of motion such as the Bloch-Redfield equation [24]. Those approaches can be extended to allow calculations of heat and work in the quantum regime [25]. However, there are several time-local equations which can be obtained, using reasonable approximations, from a given model, and these can make differing predictions for the dynamics [26,27]. This problem has been addressed by several groups, who argue that the Bloch-Redfield equation [10,26,28–33] is useful and indeed accurate, despite its potential pathologies [34]. In this paper, we extend such studies to explore the heat flows in a simple laser cooling process, with the aim of identifying an approximate time-local equation that can accurately model them.

In the following, we first review the derivation of the Bloch-Redfield equation for an open quantum system, and outline its extension to calculate heat flows. We also discuss two other time-local equations which can be obtained by making further approximations: a Lindblad form in the energy eigenbasis, obtained by making the secular approximation, and a Lindblad form in the eigenbasis of the undriven system. We use these forms to calculate the cooling spectrum, i.e., the cooling power as a function of driving frequency, in a model of laser cooling. The model allows for strong driving and includes a spectral structure for the environment. We find that a complete description of the cooling spectrum, which covers both the weak-driving and strong-driving regimes, can be achieved using the full Bloch-Redfield equation. We provide further support for the correctness of the Bloch-Redfield master equation—whose use has been controversial because it does not guarantee positivity [34], and can lead to behavior inconsistent with thermodynamic principles [35]—by comparing its predictions to those of an exact numerical method. Our conclusions support the use of Bloch-Redfield equations to model laser cooling and other thermodynamic processes [10,30,32,33,36,37].

2. Materials and Methods

2.1. Laser Cooling Model

We consider a simple laser-cooling scheme, depicted in Figure 1, involving an impurity with two states forming a ground-state manifold, and a single state in an excited-state manifold. A driving laser of frequency ω_l excites the transition from the upper state of the ground-state manifold to an excited state $|e\rangle$ and energy E_0 above the top of the ground-state manifold. We assume this state decays by radiative emission to the ground state. Crucially, the two states within the ground-state manifold, $|g_l\rangle$, $|g_u\rangle$, which are split by an energy E_{man}, are coupled by the emission and absorption of lattice phonons.

We will analyze this problem within the standard framework of open quantum systems theory, separating it into parts corresponding to a 'system', one or more baths, and the interactions between the system and the baths. In our case, the baths are the phonons, and the continuum of photon modes that give the radiative decay. We describe those aspects of the model in Section 2.4 below. The system, meanwhile, comprises the states of the impurity and their interaction with the laser, which can be treated as a classical driving field [38]. The system Hamiltonian is then ($\hbar = 1$)

$$H_S = E_0|e\rangle\langle e| - E_{man}|g_l\rangle\langle g_l| + \Omega\cos(\omega_l t)(|g_u\rangle\langle e| + |e\rangle\langle g_u|),$$

where Ω is the Rabi frequency given by the product of the electric field amplitude of the driving laser and the dipole moment of the transition, $d.E_0$. The time-dependence of the driving field can be removed, in the rotating wave approximation, by using a unitary transformation

$$U = \exp(i\omega_l t|e\rangle\langle e|). \qquad (1)$$

In this frame the driving field is time-independent, and the Hamiltonian for the system is

$$H_S = \begin{pmatrix} -\delta & \Omega/2 & 0 \\ \Omega/2 & 0 & 0 \\ 0 & 0 & -E_{man} \end{pmatrix}. \quad (2)$$

Here $\delta = \omega_l - E_0$ denotes the driving laser frequency relative to the transition. The diagonal terms in Equation (2) are the energies of the electronic states, in the rotating frame. The off-diagonal terms are the coupling between those states produced by the electric-dipole interaction with the driving field [38]. The coupling between the impurity states and the lattice phonons is considered in the following, where we discuss master equations for open quantum systems and specify the system-bath interaction Hamiltonian.

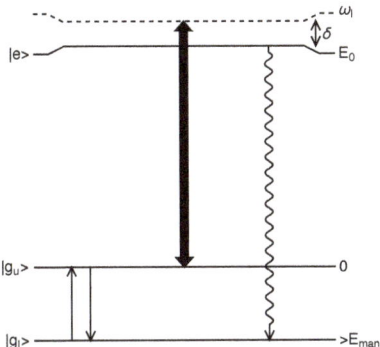

Figure 1. Energy levels of an impurity in a model laser-cooling process. The two states of a ground-state manifold, $|g_u\rangle$, and $|g_l\rangle$, are coupled by the emission and absorption of lattice phonons (vertical solid lines). Laser driving occurs on the transition from the upper level of the ground-state manifold to an excited state $|e\rangle$ (block arrow). This state decays radiatively to the ground state (wavy arrow).

2.2. Master Equations for Open Quantum Systems

Figure 1 depicts an open quantum system: one which interacts, explicitly or implicitly, with a wider environment. These interactions lead to an exchange of energy between system and environment, and dephasing and decoherence effects. Here, we have an environment comprising the phonons in the host crystal of the impurity and the photons associated with the radiative decay of the upper level.

The dynamics of an open quantum system can, in certain circumstances, be described by a time-local master equation for its reduced density matrix [24]. Such equations can be obtained from microscopic models which consider the environment explicitly in making the weak-coupling and Markovian approximations. They are also often postulated phenomenologically, based on the observation that the most general equation of motion is one of Lindblad form. However, there are several different forms of equations that can result from a microscopic model, depending on the details of the approximations made. The predictions of these forms can, furthermore, differ from those based on phenomenological Lindblad forms.

These issues have been discussed in previous works [26,28] which suggest that the full Bloch-Redfield equation—obtained by using the weak-coupling and Markovian approximations, but without making the secular approximation—gives a good description of the dynamics. This is in spite of the fact that the Bloch-Redfield equation does not guarantee that the eigenvalues of the reduced density matrix remain positive [24,34]. For a system where there are no degeneracies, or near-degeneracies, that issue can be cured by secularization [34,39], which corresponds to eliminating oscillating terms in the dissipator that average to zero over time. This leads to a Lindblad form [40,41] with positive rates. It is, however, a priori invalid for the laser-cooling protocol considered here, where weak driving near resonance means we have $\Omega \approx 0$ and $\delta \approx 0$, so that two of the eigenstates of Equation (2), $|g_u\rangle$ and $|e\rangle$, are almost degenerate in the frame where the laser field is time independent.

A fairly generic form for the Hamiltonian of an open quantum system is

$$H = H_S + H_B + H_{SB} \tag{3}$$

$$H_{SB} = \sum_k g_k O (b_k + b_k^\dagger). \tag{4}$$

Here H_S is the Hamiltonian for the system, H_B for its environment, or bath, and H_{SB} is the system-bath coupling. We consider the common situation in which the bath comprises a set of harmonic oscillators [24], which we index using a quantity or quantities labeled r. Note that r denotes the full set of quantum numbers required to label the modes. The oscillators have frequencies ω_r, and ladder operators b_r and $b_r^\dagger$. The displacement of the rth bath mode is coupled to the system operator O, with coupling strength g_r. The dissipative effects of the bath depend on its spectral density, $J(\omega) = \sum_r g_r^2 \delta(\omega - \omega_r)$.

To fix notation we recall the standard procedure for deriving a Bloch-Redfield master equation [24,42,43]. We work in the interaction picture with respect to $H_S + H_B$, so that $O(t) = e^{iH_S t} O e^{-iH_S t}$. Note that where necessary we will distinguish operators in the interaction and Schrödinger pictures as, for example, $O(t)$ and O. From the von Neumann equation we obtain the form

$$\frac{d\rho(t)}{dt} = -i[H_{SB}(t), \rho(0)] - \int_0^t dt' [H_{SB}(t), [H_{SB}(t'), \rho(t')]] \tag{5}$$

where $\rho(t)$ is the full density operator of the system and environment. For weak coupling to a bath one can replace $\rho(t') \approx \rho_S(t') \otimes \rho_B(t')$ on the right-hand side, where ρ_S is the reduced density matrix of the system, and ρ_B that of the bath. Since the bath is macroscopic it can be assumed to be unperturbed by the system, and ρ_B taken to be a thermal state at inverse temperature β. For a Markovian system one may, furthermore, approximate $\rho_S(t') \approx \rho_S(t)$. We can write the coupling operator in the eigenbasis of H_S as

$$O(t) = \sum_{ij} e^{i(E_i - E_j)t} \langle i|O|j\rangle |i\rangle\langle j| \equiv \sum_{ij} \hat{O}_{ij}(t). \tag{6}$$

Taking the trace of Equation (5) over the environment's degrees-of-freedom we find

$$\frac{d\rho_S(t)}{dt} = \sum_{ij} \{ A_{ij} [\hat{O}_{ji}(t) \rho_S(t) O(t) + O(t) \rho_S(t) \hat{O}_{ij}(t)$$
$$- \rho_S(t) \hat{O}_{ij}(t) O(t) - O(t) \hat{O}_{ji}(t) \rho_S(t)] \tag{7}$$
$$- i B_{ij} [\hat{O}_{ji}(t) \rho_S(t) O(t) - O(t) \rho_S(t) \hat{O}_{ij}(t)$$
$$+ \rho_S(t) \hat{O}_{ij}(t) O(t) - O(t) \hat{O}_{ji}(t) \rho_S(t)] \}.$$

The quantities A_{ij} and B_{ij} are related to the the real-time Green's functions of the environment at the transition frequency $\nu_{ij} = E_i - E_j$ connecting levels i and j. The quantities A_{ij} are associated with dissipation, and are

$$A_{ij} = \pi \{ [n(\nu_{ij}) + 1] J(\nu_{ij}) + n(\nu_{ji}) J(\nu_{ji}) \}. \tag{8}$$

Here $n(\nu > 0) = 1/(\exp(\beta \nu) - 1)$ is the Bose function describing the bath occupation, and $J(\nu) = 0$ for $\nu < 0$. The first term in A_{ij} corresponds to the creation of a bath quantum as the system transitions from a state i to j with $E_i - E_j > 0$, whereas the second corresponds to the absorption of a bath quantum in the opposite case, $E_i - E_j < 0$. The quantities B_{ij} are associated with energy shifts, and are given by the principal value integral

$$B_{ij} = \mathcal{P} \int J(\omega) \frac{\omega + (2n(\omega)+1)(E_i - E_j)}{\omega^2 - (E_i - E_j)^2} d\omega. \tag{9}$$

Equation (7) can be used directly, but is often further approximated, leading to other forms of equation-of-motion for an open quantum system. One very common approximation is to drop the principal value terms proportional to B_{ij}. Another common approximation is to *secularize* the equation-of-motion. This is done by decomposing the remaining coupling operators, $O(t)$, into the energy eigenbasis: $O(t) = \sum_{kl} \hat{O}_{kl}(t)$. Every term in Equation (7) then involves a product of operators corresponding to two transitions, one involving the pair of levels i and j, and one involving the pair k, l. If the levels are non-degenerate these products of operators are, in general, time-dependent in the interaction picture, and average to zero. The exception is where a transition in one direction is paired with the same transition in the opposite direction, so that the time-dependence cancels out. Retaining only those terms the dissipative part of Equation (7) becomes

$$\frac{d\rho_S(t)}{dt} = \sum_{ij} 2A_{ij}\left(\hat{O}_{ji}(t)\rho_S(t)\hat{O}_{ij}(t) - \frac{1}{2}[\rho_S(t), \hat{O}_{ij}(t)\hat{O}_{ji}(t)]_+\right), \tag{10}$$

where $[A, B]_+ = AB + BA$ is an anticommutator. This is of Lindblad form, and therefore guarantees the positivity of the density operator. It has a straightforward physical interpretation: the environment causes transitions from the system state i to the system state j at rate $2A_{ij}$.

2.3. Heat Flows from Master Equations

The method of full counting statistics [25] allows one to extend the approaches above so as to compute the heat transferred to the bath. It has been used, often with the secular approximation [44], to obtain master equations and study heat statistics in various systems, including driven quantum-dot excitons [11,15], a driven two-level system [45], a steady-state (absorption) refrigerator [10,30,36], and a two-bath spin-boson model [32,33]. The absorption refrigerator and spin-boson model have been studied using the full Bloch-Redfield approach, without the secular approximation, which highlights the role of coherences [10,30,36]. Here we give an outline of the method and present a complete form for the full counting-field Bloch-Redfield equation, which we shall use to calculate laser cooling spectra.

The heat transferred to a bath is, by definition, the change in its energy between two times. Thus we consider a process involving projective measurements of the bath energy at two times. We take the initial time to be $t_i = 0$, and suppose that at this time the system and bath are in a product state, $\rho_S(0) \otimes \rho_B$. We can then consider the probability distribution of the heat, $P(Q, t)$, which is the probability that the energy measurements of the bath at times t_i and t give results differing by Q. It is convenient also to introduce the characteristic function of the heat distribution, $\chi(u, t) = \int dQ P(Q, t)e^{iuQ}$. The variable u is known as the counting field. (This term should not be taken to imply that heat is necessarily a discrete, countable quantity. It arises from other uses of the method, such as calculations of the number of electrons transferred across a tunnel junction [25].).

One can evaluate $\chi(u, t)$ by introducing an annotated density operator, $\rho_u(t)$, such that $\chi(u, t) = \text{Tr}\,\rho_u(t)$. $\rho_u(t)$ has a non-unitary time evolution given by

$$\rho_u(t) = U_{u/2}\rho_u(0)U^\dagger_{-u/2}, \tag{11}$$

where U_u is related to the normal time-evolution operator, $U = e^{-iHt}$, by

$$U_u = e^{iuH_B}Ue^{-iuH_B}. \tag{12}$$

Note the similarity between these phase factors and the factor e^{iuQ} in the definition of the characteristic function; it is these factors that incorporate the results of the measurements of the bath energy, H_B, into $\rho_u(t)$. At the initial time the annotated density matrix is given by $\rho_u(0) = \rho(0)$.

For a general operator P we define the annotated version $P_u = e^{iuH_B}Pe^{-iuH_B}$, which obeys the Heisenberg-like equation

$$i\frac{dP_u}{du} = [P_u, H_B].$$

For the lowering operator appearing in Equation (4) we have $b_{u,k} = e^{-i\omega_k u}b_{0,k}$. Thus, the time-evolution operators, $U_{\pm u/2}$, can be obtained from the standard form, e^{-iHt}, by replacing the coupling Hamiltonian, Equation (4), with $H_{SB}^{\pm} = \sum g_k O(b_k e^{\mp i\omega u/2} + b_k^\dagger e^{\pm i\omega u/2})$.

A master equation for the reduced annotated density matrix, $\rho_{u,S}(t)$ can now be obtained, following the steps above. The essential difference is that the von Neumann equation for $\rho(t)$, in the interaction picture, must be replaced by

$$\frac{d\rho_u(t)}{dt} = -i(H_{SB}^{+}\rho_u(t) - \rho_u(t)H_{SB}^{-}). \tag{13}$$

The result is

$$\begin{aligned}\frac{d\rho_{u,S}(t)}{dt} = \sum_{ij} \{&A_{ij}[e^{iu(E_i-E_j)}(\hat{O}_{ji}(t)\rho_{u,S}(t)O(t) + O(t)\rho_{u,S}(t)\hat{O}_{ij}(t))\\ &- \rho_{u,S}(t)\hat{O}_{ij}(t)O(t) - O(t)\hat{O}_{ji}(t)\rho(t)]\\ &-iB_{ij}[e^{iu(E_i-E_j)}(\hat{O}_{ji}(t)\rho_{u,S}(t)O(t) - O(t)\rho_{u,S}(t)\hat{O}_{ij}(t))\\ &+ \rho_{u,S}(t)\hat{O}_{ij}(t)O(t) - O(t)\hat{O}_{ji}(t)\rho(t)]\}.\end{aligned} \tag{14}$$

This form differs from Equation (7) by the addition of phase factors in the four terms that cause transitions between the system eigenstates. It can be approximated as discussed above, by dropping the principal value terms, or by making the secular approximation.

The mean heat is

$$\langle Q \rangle = \int QP(Q)dQ = -i\frac{d\chi}{du}\bigg|_{u=0} = -i\operatorname{Tr}\frac{d\rho_{u,S}(t)}{du}\bigg|_{u=0}. \tag{15}$$

From Equation (14) we find that the heat current is

$$\begin{aligned}\frac{d\langle Q\rangle}{dt} = \sum_{ij}\{&A_{ij}[(E_i - E_j)\operatorname{Tr}(\hat{O}_{ji}(t)\rho_S(t)O(t) + O(t)\rho_S(t)\hat{O}_{ij}(t))]\\ &-iB_{ij}[(E_i - E_j)\operatorname{Tr}(\hat{O}_{ji}(t)\rho_S(t)O(t) - O(t)\rho_S(t)\hat{O}_{ij}(t))]\}.\end{aligned} \tag{16}$$

This can be used to calculate the heat current from the density matrix, $\rho_{u=0,S}(t) = \rho_S(t)$, obtained by solving the standard Bloch-Redfield Equation (7).

2.4. Master Equations for Laser Cooling

We consider a model in which the system Hamiltonian is given by Equation (2). We suppose that there is a continuum of phonons responsible for transitions between the states of the ground-state manifold. This phonon bath will be described by Equations (3) and (4), with coupling operator $O = |g_l\rangle\langle g_u| + |g_u\rangle\langle g_l|$. For the spectral density of this bath, we take the super-Ohmic form with an exponential high-frequency cut-off, $J(\omega) = 2\alpha(\omega^3/\omega_c^2)\exp(-\omega/\omega_c)$. We are not targetting a detailed model of a real system, and this form is chosen largely for illustrative purposes. It may, however, be noted that it corresponds to that for acoustic phonons coupling to localized impurities such as the silicon-vacancy center in diamond [22] or a quantum-dot exciton [20]. α is a dimensionless measure of the coupling strength, and ω_c is a high-frequency cut-off. Such cut-offs arise from the size of the electronic states and correspond roughly to the phonon frequency at a wavelength given by that size.

We also consider, in the following, an alternative form of dissipator, of standard Lindblad form. For a transition caused by a jump operator A, with rate γ_A, the standard Lindblad form is

$$\frac{d\rho_S(t)}{dt} = \gamma_A \mathcal{L}_A \rho_S(t) = \gamma_A \left(A \rho_S(t) A^\dagger - \frac{1}{2}[\rho_S(t), A^\dagger A]_+ \right). \tag{17}$$

Thus the natural phenomenological form, capturing the processes shown in Figure 1, is to combine two of these dissipative terms, one for phonon absorption, with rate γ_+ and jump operator $\sigma_+ = |g_u\rangle\langle g_l|$, and one for phonon emission, with rate γ_- and jump operator $\sigma_- = \sigma_+^\dagger = |g_l\rangle\langle g_u|$. Such a form corresponds to Equation (10) when the eigenstates of H_S are simply $|g_l\rangle$ and $|g_u\rangle$, which is resonable for weak driving. This comparison allows us to identify the appropriate rates, from Equation (8), as $\gamma_- = 2\pi(n(E_{man})+1)J(E_{man})$ and $\gamma_+ = 2\pi n(E_{man})J(E_{man})$.

In addition to the phonon dissipation, our model involves the radiative decay of the excited state, $|e\rangle$ to the ground state $|g_l\rangle$. We model this as a Lindblad form with jump operator $|g_l\rangle\langle e|$, and rate γ.

2.5. Exact Methods

As well as results of master equations, we shall present, in the following, calculations of the heat flows obtained by numerically-exact simulations [46–48] of the model open quantum system described above. The technique, known as TEMPO, calculates the path integral for the evolution of an open quantum system, discretizing time into a series of steps [49]. It uses a matrix-product state representation to efficiently store the augmented density tensor, which allows it to consider large memory times for the bath [47,48]. Combining path-integral methods with the counting-field technique [32,46], allows calculations of the total heat transferred to the phonon bath up to a particular time. Details of the method, and the associated code, are given in Ref. [46]. We use it to calculate the heat currents to the phonons by taking the difference of the total heat transferred to the bath between two times, separated by a single timestep. In these calculations, the dynamics of the system and the effects of the phonon bath are treated exactly. We do not treat the radiative decay in this first-principles fashion, but rather include it using the same Lindblad form we use for the master equation approach. We believe this is appropriate, in as much as the bath associated with radiative decay has no spectral structure, in contrast with that associated with the phonons. The TEMPO approach has recently been extended to simulations with multiple baths [50], which would allow it to treat laser cooling with structured photon environments, e.g., in optical resonators.

3. Results

The parameters in our model are the energy splitting of the ground-state manifold, the detuning and Rabi frequency of the driving, the radiative decay rate, γ, the cut-off frequency, ω_c, the dimensionless coupling, α, and the temperature T. We choose the energy and time units such that $E_{man} = 2$. For the remaining parameters we take $\gamma = 0.5$, $\omega_c = 1$, $\alpha = 0.01$, and $T = 3$. These parameters are not intended to be realistic but are chosen to allow us to compute the exact solutions with a reasonable effort, and compare the results of the different master equations. In particular, we choose a large value for the radiative decay rate, γ, to increase the magnitude of the heat current. It may be noted that for these parameters the phonon absorption rate, $\gamma_+ \approx 0.14$, is comparable to, but smaller than, the radiative decay rate. This differs from the situation for conventional laser cooling, appropriate in systems such as rare-earth ions, where the phonon rates are much larger than those for radiative decay [1], and the electronic populations are very close to equilibrium. It implies that, in our case, the heat current will be limited by the driving strength (for weak driving) or the phonon rate (for strong driving), and not the radiative lifetime.

Figure 2 shows the calculating cooling power as a function of the detuning, δ, for four different strengths of the driving field. The different curves are computed using the full Bloch-Redfield equation, (7), the phenomenological Lindblad form, Equation (17), and the secular Bloch-Redfield equation, (10). Considering first weak driving, in Figure 2a, we see that the Bloch-Redfield and phenomenological theories agree well, and give a cooling profile that appears to be Lorentzian, as one would expect. While the secular Bloch-Redfield equation agrees away from the resonance, we see that it fails close to it, massively overestimating the cooling power. The secular approximation is, of course, not justified here, because there are near degeneracies in the Hamiltonian. Nonetheless, the level of disagreement seems surprising, given the agreement away from resonance.

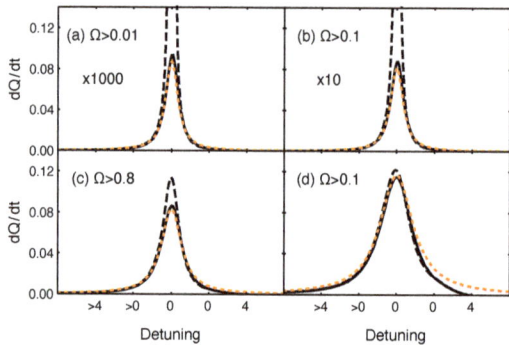

Figure 2. Rates of heat absorption from the phonon bath, as a function of the detuning $\delta = \omega_l - E_0$ of the driving laser from resonance, for four different Rabi frequencies. For each Rabi frequency, we show results computed using the full Bloch-Redfield equation (solid black curve), a phenomenological Lindblad equation (dashed orange curve), and the Bloch-Redfield equation in the secular approximation without the principal value terms (dashed black curve). The Rabi frequencies Ω are: (**a**) 0.01, (**b**) 0.1, (**c**) 0.5, and (**d**) 1.0.

In the converse, strong-driving region, Figure 2d, all three methods give similar results. However, there is a noticeable difference on the high-energy side of the transition, with the phenomenological theory giving, as before, a Lorentzian profile, while the other theories predict the heat current drops off more rapidly, and indeed switches direction, from cooling to heating, in the range of detunings shown.

Figure 3 shows the temperature dependence of the cooling power for weak resonant driving. As noted above, the secular approximation is inappropriate in this regime and massively overestimates the cooling power. The other theories agree closely and appear physically reasonable, predicting that the cooling power drops rapidly once the temperature is lowered below the splitting E_{man}. This is the expected physical behavior for laser cooling in a discrete level structure, caused by the vanishing of the phonon occupation at temperatures much less than E_{man}. The precise behavior at very low temperatures is not relevant to laser cooling since it is not expected to operate there. Nonetheless, it may be noted that, for these parameters, the Bloch-Redfield theory predicts a very small but negative cooling power, i.e., net heating, at very low temperatures ($T < 0.38$). However, this is an approximate theory whose accuracy is not sufficient to discern the true behavior of the heat current in this regime. Indeed, we find that at these very low temperatures the theory does not predict a physical density matrix, giving one which has a negative, albeit very small, eigenvalue.

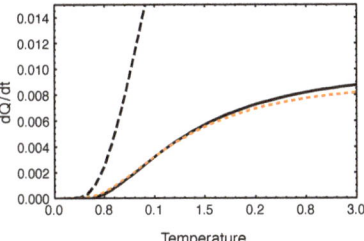

Figure 3. Rate of heat absorption from the phonon bath, as a function of temperature, for the different approaches. Results are shown for weak driving, $\Omega = 0.1$, at resonance, $\delta = 0$. The heat current is computed using the full Bloch-Redfield equation (solid black curve), the phenomenological Lindblad equation (dashed orange curve), and the Bloch-Redfield equation in the secular approximation without the principal value terms (dashed black curve).

In Figure 4 we compare the cooling spectra predicted by the full Bloch-Redfield equation with those obtained from the exact numerical method [46]. The numerical method simulates the time-evolution of the open quantum system, using discrete timesteps. For these simulations, we have taken a timestep $dt = 0.05$, and computed the heat current, at a time $t = 30.0$, from the difference in the heat transfer at two times. The mean heat transfer is computed by evaluating the annotated reduced density matrix, $\rho_{u,S}(t)$, and computing the finite difference approximation to the derivative in Equation (15) from the values of Tr $\rho_{u,S}(t)$ at $u = 0.05$ and $u = 0.0$. The numerical accuracy and convergence of these simulations involve two further parameters: a maximum number of timesteps retained in the influence functional, K, and a cut-off parameter controlling the truncation of the singular-value decompositions. We take $K = 100$, and use a cut-off of 10^{-7}.

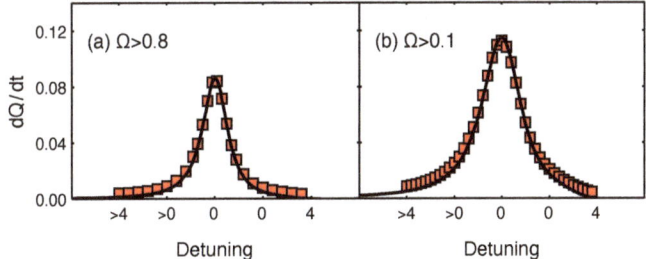

Figure 4. Heat absorption rates, as a function of the detuning, computed using the full Bloch-Redfield equation (solid black curves) and a numerically exact method (red squares), for two different Rabi frequencies. The Rabi frequencies Ω are (**a**) 0.5 and (**b**) 1.0.

We see from Figure 4 that the Bloch-Redfield equation is in excellent agreement with the numerical results. The non-Lorentzian behavior of the cooling profile on the high-energy side, predicted by the full Bloch-Redfield and secular equations, is present. There is a slight overestimate of the cooling power in the tails of the profiles, which we believe is because of the heat current has not yet reached its steady-state value at those small values of the cooling power.

4. Discussion

Figures 2 and 4 suggest that the full Bloch-Redfield equation gives an accurate account of the cooling profile, in both the weak- and strong-driving cases. In the weak-driving case, it agrees with the phenomenological theory, which is well-justified for weak-driving, while in the strong-driving case it agrees with the secular theory, which is well-justified there. Furthermore, it agrees with exact numerical results, in the strong-driving regime where such simulations are possible. Thus the Bloch-Redfield equation allows a complete treatment of both regimes, using a single equation. This conclusion is similar to previous conclusions on the dynamics and thermodynamics of other open quantum systems, where the Bloch-Redfield equation has similarly been argued to provide the most accurate description [10,26,28–30]. This is in spite of the possibility that it produces unphysical density matrices with non-positive eigenvalues. That possibility does not occur in our results, except at very low temperatures where laser cooling would not, in any case, be expected to operate.

In previous works, it has been noted that the secular approximation does not allow for the presence of bath-induced or noise-induced coherence [51] in multilevel systems where near-degenerate levels have different couplings to the bath [26]. This phenomenon can play an important role for the heat currents, as has been pointed out previously for quantum absorption refrigerators [10,30]. Its significance in our case can be seen by comparing the secular result (where there is no bath-induced coherence) and the Bloch-Redfield result (where there is) in Figure 2. When $\delta = 0, \Omega = 0$ our Hamiltonian has two degenerate eigenstates, but the form of those eigenstates depends on how the limit is taken: for $\delta = 0, \Omega \neq 0$ they are $|\pm\rangle = |g_u\rangle \pm |e\rangle$, but for $\Omega = 0, \delta \neq 0$ they are $|g_u\rangle$ and $|e\rangle$. The naive form of secular approximation in Equation (10) produces a dissipator which populates the states $|+\rangle$ and $|-\rangle$, and destroys coherences between them. However, we observe that the phonon bath couples only to $|g_u\rangle \propto |+\rangle + |-\rangle$, and not to $|e\rangle \propto |+\rangle - |-\rangle$, so in the weak-driving case the correct dissipator should affect the population of the first combination, while leaving that of the second undamped. This means that there are undamped coherences in the $|\pm\rangle$ basis, which survive in the steady-state [26], and produce corrections to the heat currents relative to the results of the secular approximation.

Author Contributions: Conceptualization, methodology, software, analysis, investigation, C.N.M., L.T.T. and P.R.E. Writing—original draft preparation, P.R.E.; writing—review and editing, C.N.M. and L.T.T.; visualization, supervision, P.R.E. All authors have read and agreed to the published version of the manuscript.

Funding: This research was funded by the Irish Research Council grant number GOIPG/2017/1091. Some calculations were performed on the Boyle cluster maintained by the Trinity Centre for High-Performance Computing. This cluster was funded through grants from the European Research Council and Science Foundation Ireland.

Institutional Review Board Statement: Not applicable.

Informed Consent Statement: Not applicable.

Data Availability Statement: The data generated in this study are available in Zenodo at https://doi.org/10.5281/zenodo.5715836 (accessed on 18 November 2021).

Acknowledgments: We thank D. Segal for helpful comments on the manuscript, and G. Fux, B. Lovett, and J. Keeling for discussions and assistance with the TEMPO and PT-TEMPO codes.

Conflicts of Interest: The authors declare no conflict of interest.

References

1. Seletskiy, D.V.; Epstein, R.; Sheik-Bahae, M. Laser Cooling in Solids: Advances and Prospects. *Rep. Prog. Phys.* **2016**, *79*, 096401. [CrossRef] [PubMed]
2. Nemova, G.; Kashyap, R. Laser Cooling of Solids. *Rep. Prog. Phys.* **2010**, *73*, 086501. [CrossRef]
3. Epstein, R.; Sheik-Bahae, M. (Eds.) *Optical Refrigeration: Science and Applications of Laser Cooling of Solids*, 1st ed.; Wiley: Hoboken, NJ, USA, 2009. [CrossRef]
4. Scovil, H.E.D.; Schulz-DuBois, E.O. Three-Level Masers as Heat Engines. *Phys. Rev. Lett.* **1959**, *2*, 262–263. [CrossRef]
5. Geusic, J.E.; Schulz-DuBios, E.O.; Scovil, H.E.D. Quantum Equivalent of the Carnot Cycle. *Phys. Rev.* **1967**, *156*, 343–351. [CrossRef]
6. Linden, N.; Popescu, S.; Skrzypczyk, P. How Small Can Thermal Machines Be? The Smallest Possible Refrigerator. *Phys. Rev. Lett.* **2010**, *105*, 130401. [CrossRef]

8. Creatore, C.; Parker, M.A.; Emmott, S.; Chin, A.W. Efficient Biologically Inspired Photocell Enhanced by Delocalized Quantum States. *Phys. Rev. Lett.* **2013**, *111*, 253601. [CrossRef]
9. Fruchtman, A.; Gómez-Bombarelli, R.; Lovett, B.W.; Gauger, E.M. Photocell Optimization Using Dark State Protection. *Phys. Rev. Lett.* **2016**, *117*, 203603. [CrossRef]
10. Dorfman, K.E.; Xu, D.; Cao, J. Efficiency at Maximum Power of Laser Quantum Heat Engine Enhanced by Noise-Induced Coherence. *Phys. Rev. E* **2018**, *97*, 042120. [CrossRef]
11. Kilgour, M.; Segal, D. Coherence and Decoherence in Quantum Absorption Refrigerators. *Phys. Rev. E* **2018**, *98*, 012117. [CrossRef]
12. Murphy, C.N.; Eastham, P.R. Quantum Control of Excitons for Reversible Heat Transfer. *Commun. Phys.* **2019**, *2*, 120. [CrossRef]
13. Brash, A.J.; Martins, L.M.P.P.; Barth, A.M.; Liu, F.; Quilter, J.H.; Glässl, M.; Axt, V.M.; Ramsay, A.J.; Skolnick, M.S.; Fox, A.M. Dynamic Vibronic Coupling in InGaAs Quantum Dots. *J. Opt. Soc. Am. B* **2016**, *33*, C115–C122. [CrossRef]
14. Eastham, P.R.; Spracklen, A.O.; Keeling, J. Lindblad Theory of Dynamical Decoherence of Quantum-Dot Excitons. *Phys. Rev. B* **2013**, *87*, 195306. [CrossRef]
15. Ramsay, A.J.; Gopal, A.V.; Gauger, E.M.; Nazir, A.; Lovett, B.W.; Fox, A.M.; Skolnick, M.S. Damping of Exciton Rabi Rotations by Acoustic Phonons in Optically Excited InGaAs/GaAs Quantum Dots. *Phys. Rev. Lett.* **2010**, *104*, 017402. [CrossRef]
16. Gauger, E.M.; Wabnig, J. Heat Pumping with Optically Driven Excitons. *Phys. Rev. B* **2010**, *82*, 073301. [CrossRef]
17. Abiuso, P.; Giovannetti, V. Non-Markov Enhancement of Maximum Power for Quantum Thermal Machines. *Phys. Rev. A* **2019**, *99*, 052106. [CrossRef]
18. Thomas, G.; Siddharth, N.; Banerjee, S.; Ghosh, S. Thermodynamics of Non-Markovian Reservoirs and Heat Engines. *Phys. Rev. E* **2018**, *97*, 062108. [CrossRef] [PubMed]
19. Bylicka, B.; Tukiainen, M.; Chruściński, D.; Piilo, J.; Maniscalco, S. Thermodynamic Power of Non-Markovianity. *Sci. Rep.* **2016**, *6*, 27989. [CrossRef]
20. Correa, L.A.; Palao, J.P.; Alonso, D.; Adesso, G. Quantum-Enhanced Absorption Refrigerators. *Sci. Rep.* **2015**, *4*, 3949. [CrossRef] [PubMed]
21. Nazir, A.; McCutcheon, D.P.S. Modelling Exciton–Phonon Interactions in Optically Driven Quantum Dots. *J. Phys. Condens. Matter* **2016**, *28*, 103002. [CrossRef] [PubMed]
22. Wrachtrup, J.; Jelezko, F. Processing Quantum Information in Diamond. *J. Phys. Condens. Matter* **2006**, *18*, S807–S824. [CrossRef]
23. Norambuena, A.; Reyes, S.A.; Mejía-Lopéz, J.; Gali, A.; Maze, J.R. Microscopic Modeling of the Effect of Phonons on the Optical Properties of Solid-State Emitters. *Phys. Rev. B* **2016**, *94*, 134305. [CrossRef]
24. Basilewitsch, D.; Cosco, F.; Lo Gullo, N.; Möttönen, M.; Ala-Nissilä, T.; Koch, C.P.; Maniscalco, S. Reservoir Engineering Using Quantum Optimal Control for Qubit Reset. *New J. Phys.* **2019**, *21*, 093054. [CrossRef]
25. Breuer, H.P.; Petruccione, F. *The Theory of Open Quantum Systems*; Oxford University Press: Oxford, UK, 2002.
26. Esposito, M.; Harbola, U.; Mukamel, S. Nonequilibrium Fluctuations, Fluctuation Theorems, and Counting Statistics in Quantum Systems. *Rev. Mod. Phys.* **2009**, *81*, 1665–1702. [CrossRef]
27. Eastham, P.R.; Kirton, P.; Cammack, H.M.; Lovett, B.W.; Keeling, J. Bath-Induced Coherence and the Secular Approximation. *Phys. Rev. A* **2016**, *94*, 012110. [CrossRef]
28. Hofer, P.P.; Perarnau-Llobet, M.; Miranda, L.D.M.; Haack, G.; Silva, R.; Brask, J.B.; Brunner, N. Markovian Master Equations for Quantum Thermal Machines: Local versus Global Approach. *New J. Phys.* **2017**, *19*, 123037. [CrossRef]
29. Hartmann, R.; Strunz, W.T. Accuracy Assessment of Perturbative Master Equations: Embracing Nonpositivity. *Phys. Rev. A* **2020**, *101*, 012103. [CrossRef]
30. Purkayastha, A.; Dhar, A.; Kulkarni, M. Out-of-Equilibrium Open Quantum Systems: A Comparison of Approximate Quantum Master Equation Approaches with Exact Results. *Phys. Rev. A* **2016**, *93*, 062114. [CrossRef]
31. Liu, J.; Segal, D. Coherences and the Thermodynamic Uncertainty Relation: Insights from Quantum Absorption Refrigerators. *Phys. Rev. E* **2021**, *103*, 032138. [CrossRef]
32. Jeske, J.; Ing, D.J.; Plenio, M.B.; Huelga, S.F.; Cole, J.H. Bloch-Redfield Equations for Modeling Light-Harvesting Complexes. *J. Chem. Phys.* **2015**, *142*, 064104. [CrossRef]
33. Kilgour, M.; Agarwalla, B.K.; Segal, D. Path-Integral Methodology and Simulations of Quantum Thermal Transport: Full Counting Statistics Approach. *J. Chem. Phys.* **2019**, *150*, 084111. [CrossRef]
34. Boudjada, N.; Segal, D. From Dissipative Dynamics to Studies of Heat Transfer at the Nanoscale: Analysis of the Spin-Boson Model. *J. Phys. Chem. A* **2014**, *118*, 11323–11336. [CrossRef] [PubMed]
35. Dümcke, R.; Spohn, H. The Proper Form of the Generator in the Weak Coupling Limit. *Z. Phys. B* **1979**, *34*, 419–422. [CrossRef]
36. González, J.O.; Correa, L.A.; Nocerino, G.; Palao, J.P.; Alonso, D.; Adesso, G. Testing the Validity of the 'Local' and 'Global' GKLS Master Equations on an Exactly Solvable Model. *Open Syst. Inf. Dyn.* **2017**, *24*, 1740010. [CrossRef]
37. Friedman, H.M.; Agarwalla, B.K.; Segal, D. Quantum Energy Exchange and Refrigeration: A Full-Counting Statistics Approach. *New J. Phys.* **2018**, *20*, 083026. [CrossRef]
38. Trushechkin, A.S.; Merkli, M.; Cresser, J.D.; Anders, J. Open Quantum System Dynamics and the Mean Force Gibbs State. *arXiv* **2021**, arXiv:2110.01671.
39. Allen, L.; Eberly, J.H. *Optical Resonance and Two-Level Atoms*; Dover Publications: New York, NY, USA, 1987.
40. Wangsness, R.K.; Bloch, F. The Dynamical Theory of Nuclear Induction. *Phys. Rev.* **1953**, *89*, 728–739. [CrossRef]

40. Lindblad, G. On the Generators of Quantum Dynamical Semigroups. *Commun. Math. Phys.* **1976**, *48*, 119–130. [CrossRef]
41. Gorini, V.; Kossakowski, A.; Sudarshan, E.C.G. Completely Positive Dynamical Semigroups of N-level Systems. *J. Math. Phys.* **1976**, *17*, 821–825. [CrossRef]
42. Redfield, A.G. On the Theory of Relaxation Processes. *IBM J. Res. Dev.* **1957**, *1*, 19–31. [CrossRef]
43. Bloch, F. Generalized Theory of Relaxation. *Phys. Rev.* **1957**, *105*, 1206–1222. [CrossRef]
44. Silaev, M.; Heikkilä, T.T.; Virtanen, P. Lindblad-Equation Approach for the Full Counting Statistics of Work and Heat in Driven Quantum Systems. *Phys. Rev. E* **2014**, *90*, 022103. [CrossRef] [PubMed]
45. Gasparinetti, S.; Solinas, P.; Braggio, A.; Sassetti, M. Heat-Exchange Statistics in Driven Open Quantum Systems. *New J. Phys.* **2014**, *16*, 115001. [CrossRef]
46. Popovic, M.; Mitchison, M.T.; Strathearn, A.; Lovett, B.W.; Goold, J.; Eastham, P.R. Quantum Heat Statistics with Time-Evolving Matrix Product Operators. *PRX Quantum* **2021**, *2*, 020338. [CrossRef]
47. Strathearn, A.; Kirton, P.; Kilda, D.; Keeling, J.; Lovett, B.W. Efficient Non-Markovian Quantum Dynamics Using Time-Evolving Matrix Product Operators. *Nat. Commun.* **2018**, *9*, 3322. [CrossRef]
48. Fux, G.E.; Butler, E.P.; Eastham, P.R.; Lovett, B.W.; Keeling, J. Efficient Exploration of Hamiltonian Parameter Space for Optimal Control of Non-Markovian Open Quantum Systems. *Phys. Rev. Lett.* **2021**, *126*, 200401. [CrossRef] [PubMed]
49. Makri, N.; Makarov, D.E. Tensor Propagator for Iterative Quantum Time Evolution of Reduced Density Matrices. II. Numerical Methodology. *J. Chem. Phys.* **1995**, *102*, 4611–4618. [CrossRef]
50. Gribben, D.; Rouse, D.M.; Iles-Smith, J.; Strathearn, A.; Maguire, H.; Kirton, P.; Nazir, A.; Gauger, E.M.; Lovett, B.W. Exact Dynamics of Non-Additive Environments in Non-Markovian Open Quantum Systems. *arXiv* **2021**, arXiv:2109.08442.
51. Tscherbul, T.V.; Brumer, P. Long-Lived Quasistationary Coherences in a V-type System Driven by Incoherent Light. *Phys. Rev. Lett.* **2014**, *113*, 113601. [CrossRef]

MDPI
St. Alban-Anlage 66
4052 Basel
Switzerland
Tel. +41 61 683 77 34
Fax +41 61 302 89 18
www.mdpi.com

Applied Sciences Editorial Office
E-mail: applsci@mdpi.com
www.mdpi.com/journal/applsci

www.ingramcontent.com/pod-product-compliance
Lightning Source LLC
LaVergne TN
LVHW070542100526
838202LV00012B/356